The Limits of Computing

The Jones and Bartlett Series in Computer Science

Bernstein, A. J., and Lewis, P. M.,
  Concurrency in Programming and Database Systems

Chandy, K. M., and Taylor, S.,
  An Introduction to Parallel Programming

Flynn, M. J.,
  Processor Design

Lee, E. S.,
  Algorithms and Data Structures in Computer Engineering

Walker, H. M.,
  The Limits of Computing

The Limits of Computing

Henry M. Walker

Department of Mathematics and Computer Science
Grinnell College

JONES AND BARTLETT PUBLISHERS
BOSTON   LONDON

Editorial, Sales, and Customer Service Offices
Jones and Bartlett Publishers
One Exeter Plaza
Boston, MA 02116
1-800-832-0034
1-617-859-3900

Jones and Bartlett Publishers International
P.O. Box 1498
London W6 7RS
England

Library of Congress Cataloging-in-Publication Data

Walker, Henry M.,   1947–
    The Limits of Computing / Henry M. Walker
        p.   cm.
    Includes bibliographical references and index.
    ISBN 0-86720-206-8
    1. Electronic data processing   I. Title.
    QA76.W185   1994   92-18211
    004--dc20   CIP

Excerpts on the opening page of Chapter 10 are reprinted with the permission of Science Research Associates, an imprint of MacMillan Publishing Company, Inc., from the *The Compleat Computer, Second Edition*, Dennie Van Tassel and Cynthia L. Van Tassel. Copyright © 1983 by Science Research Associates.

Printed in the United States of America
97 96 95 94 93   10 9 8 7 6 5 4 3 2 1

Contents

8. Human Factors   133

9. Security Issues   159

Preface

The success of computers is widely recognized. Computers are used in a vast array of applications, and the press publicizes new applications and breakthroughs virtually every week. This spectacular track record has supported a common perspective that computers can do anything, given sufficient development time and resources. This view is reinforced by many introductory computing books, which might be characterized as following a "gee-whiz" view of technology, and each chapter may discuss another "nifty" application of computers. With this perspective, discussions rarely pay any attention to possible limitations of computing.

This book presents another side of computing by considering a wide range of factors that constrain the use of computers. Some limitations are practical – problems may be too complex to specify precisely or to solve. Other constraints are theoretical – some problems are known to be unsolvable, while others have solutions that cannot be completed in any reasonable amount of time. Security and personnel considerations present additional complicating factors. While this discussion of limitations does not reduce the range of successes that have been achieved with computers, issues raised here are vital to any balanced view of computing.

═══ MAIN FEATURES ═══

The presentation of topics in this text includes many features designed to make this material accessible, understandable, and interesting.

- *Few Prerequisites*
  Discussions are self contained; the text does not assume that the reader has considerable computing or programming background.

- *Depth of Coverage*
  Topics are discussed in some reasonable depth; discussions are not watered down or glossed over, contrary to treatments found in many introductory-level books. For example, chapter 4 outlines a proof that the Halting Problem is unsolvable.

- *Discussion of Provocative Topics*
  The text addresses both practical constraints and theoretical limitations.

In addition, questions at the end of each chapter suggest directions for further exploration and consideration.

- *Appropriate at Many Levels*
  With its combination of few prerequisites and depth, this book is appropriate for a wide range of people who have some interest in computing. For example, the material covered here is appropriate for most high school or college students, for managers or bureaucrats who make policy decisions involving computing, and for professionals with an interest in philosophical or ethical issues of computing.

- *Rather Light, Informal Style*
  The prose is written in a down-to-earth, relaxed style, which is designed to be fun. The text contains relevant cartoons, non-technical stories, and anecdotes. Readers expecting a dry, dense, jargon-laden style will be disappointed. (Do not use this book if your goal is to be lulled to sleep.)

- *Examples*
  Abstract ideas and principles are illustrated by a large number of examples, many reviewing actual experiences and events.

AUDIENCE

As noted above, this book has few prerequisites and is aimed for general audiences. As such, it can serve effectively as an adjunct to courses in computer literacy and in various CS1 and CS2 courses. This book also supports recent trends to incorporate social and ethical issues into the computing curriculum in a meaningful way. (Thus, this book can reinforce *Computing Curricula 1991* from the ACM and IEEE in a variety of ways.) With the widespread importance and application of the topics discussed, this book also will appeal to any person with a general interest in computing.

COPYRIGHTED MATERIALS

Material in this book includes some text, tables, figures, and cartoons that have been copyrighted previously. While some of this work is cited under the Fair Use clauses of the copyright laws, special acknowledgment is made for some specific materials.

Trademarks Acknowledgment is made of the following trademarks.

EMBOS is a registered trademark of ELXSI.

UNIX is a registered trademark of AT&T UNIX System Laboratories.

VMS is a registered trademark of Digital Equipment Corporation.

VM-TSO is a registered trademark of International Business Machines Corporation.

Credits for Part and Chapter Openings. The author gratefully acknowledges the permissions received for various chapter and part openings from the following individuals and publishers.

Part I – "I hear they're doing some amazing things with computers these days." Cartoon: Steve Attoe.

Chapter 1 – "I thought computers took care of this." Don Orehek, *Compute*, Volume 13, Number 9, Issue 133, September 1991, p. 99.

Part II – From: *MATHEMATICS: PROBLEM SOLVING THROUGH RECREATIONAL MATHEMATICS* by: Bonnie Averbach and Orin Chein. Copyright © 1980 by W.H. Freeman and Co. Reprinted by permission.

Chapter 2 – Cartoon: Mathew Guss.

Chapter 3 – *Maine Sampler,* a Collection of Maine Humor by Bill Sawyer. Published by Down East Books, Camden, Maine, 1986.

Chapter 4 – *Maine Sampler,* a Collection of Maine Humor by Bill Sawyer. Published by Down East Books, Camden, Maine, 1986.

Part III – "Next Week's Lesson ..." cited in Bill Howard, "Abort, Retry, Fail?" *PC Magazine*, Volume 11, Number 6, March 31, 1992, p. 454.

Chapter 5 – From Nathaniel Borenstein, *Programming As If People Mattered*, Princeton University Press, 1991, p. 37.

Part IV – Sidney Harris "It goes on to say, 'The fault isn't with the hardware. It's with you–the software'."

Chapter 7 – *The Oxford English Dictionary*, Second Edition, Oxford University Press, New York, and Clarendon Press, 1989, by permission of Oxford University Press.

Chapter 9 – "Forget straw-into-gold, I just put a cool million in your bank account." Mathew Guss, *Datamation,* November 1, 1990, p. 60.

Part V – Anonymous ATM graffiti, quoted by Bryan Kocher, *Communications of the ACM*, Volume 32, Number 6, June 1989, p. 660; and from standard disclaimer of a major software vendor, reported by the Computer Professionals for Social Responsibility, P. O. Box 717, Palo Alto, CA 94301.

Chapter 10 – "A Dead Fish," Reprinted with the permission of Science Research Associates, an imprint of Macmillan Publishing Company, Inc. from *The Compleat Computer, Second Edition*, by Dennie Van Tassel and Cynthia L. Van Tassel. Copyright © 1983 by Science Research Associates, p. 22.

"Piano Sale," Reprinted with the permission of Science Research Associates, an imprint of Macmillan Publishing Company, Inc. from *The Compleat Computer, Second Edition*, by Dennie Van Tassel and Cynthia L. Van Tassel. Copyright © 1983 by Science Research Associates, p. 233.

Credits for Tables and Figures. Similarly, permission to use the following materials is gratefully acknowledged.

Excerpt, p. 39 – The "Barber of Seville" was originally stated by Bertrand Russell. The account here is taken from page 16 of Martin Gardner's *aha! Gotcha*, W. H. Freeman and Company, San Francisco, California, 1982.

Figure 5.3 – "This time I definitely think it's a hardware problem." Andrew Toos, *Datamation*, June 1, 1992, p. 60.

Excerpt, p. 82 – "Development of the Handley Page Victor jet bomber" Reported in *Software Engineering Notes*, Volume 11, Number 2, April 1986, p. 12, corrected by *Software Engineering Notes*, Volume 11, Number 3, July 1986, p. 25.

Figure 9.1 – Clifford Stoll, "Stalking the Wily Hacker," *Communications of the ACM*, Volume 31, Number 5, May 1988, p. 487.

Figure 10.1 – Poster by the Computer Professionals for Social Responsibility, P. O. Box 717, Palo Alto, California 94301.

═══ THANKS ═══

The development of this book has been greatly aided by the contribution of many people, and the author would like to express his deep thanks to all those who helped. First, the author wishes to thank Carl Hesler and Jones and Bartlett Publishers for their interest, support, and guidance in this project. Second, the author also thanks David Mallis at Publishing Experts, Inc., for his wonderful work in designing this book and in producing appropriate TeX macros to implement this design.

Many parts of this text have benefited greatly from reviews of many people, including Barbara Owens, Trinity University, and Rhys Price Jones, Oberlin College. Additional comments and helpful suggestions were received from students who read drafts of several chapters as part of two tutorial classes at Grinnell College. The author also expresses his appreciation to Vikram Subramaniam for his helpful comments on the manuscript and for his help with editing and secretarial work.

Next, the author gratefully acknowledges the supportive environment found during summers in the Computer Sciences Department of the University of Texas at Austin. Due to pressures during the normal academic year, drafts for most of this book were written during summer teaching appointments in Austin. Similarly, the author thanks Grinnell College for its computing and administrative support during the preparation of this manuscript. Kevin Engel, Science Librarian at Grinnell College, deserves special mention for his help tracking down answers to a variety of detailed and obscure reference questions.

Finally, I want to express my gratitude to my family, my wife Terry and my daughters Donna and Barbara, for tolerating me during the many ups and downs in writing, revising, and producing this book.

PART I
Introduction

I hear they're doing some amazing things with computers these days.

This is an exciting age. Breakthroughs in technology occur daily, science is unlocking many mysteries of the natural world, goods and services are increasingly available (making life easier), and people have more control over their environment than at any time in the past. At the same time, computers have evolved to help solve a very wide range of problems. In fact, most recent scientific and technological successes have been very dependent upon related successes in computing and computer science.

Given these impressive advances in computing, it is common to hear about ways that computers are used that capture the imagination. The news is full of stories in which computers are used in exciting ways to reach new heights. Computer literacy books and introductory courses describe a wide range of applications of computers. To achieve these successes, much difficult technical work has been required, so it is appropriate to celebrate when such work solves important problems.

Unfortunately, the publicity of the successes of technology in general and of computing in particular can also give people the impression that all problems can be solved by technology (at least with enough effort). The focus on successful efforts often ignores attempts that end in failure. (Few journals, for example, publish articles with titles such as "Thirty-Five Wrong Ways to Solve Problem X" or "Failures I Have Enjoyed." Further, if such articles did appear, it is not clear that anyone would study them.)

In the midst of this unbridled optimism about the capabilities of computers, it is important to consider whether all problems can ultimately be solved by computers. In a succinct form, the relevant questions might be:

1. What can go wrong when trying to use computers to solve problems?

2. Are there limitations on what problems computers can solve?

To put it briefly, this book answers these questions with the respective responses:

1. Almost anything.

2. Yes—many, both theoretical and practical.

The goal of this book is to expand upon these answers.

To begin, Chapter 1 reviews the problem-solving process and describes some of the major components involved in a computer solution to a problem. Subsequent chapters focus on individual pieces of this overall use of computers.

I thought computers took care of this.

Reprinted courtesy *Compute* magazine © 1991.

An Overview of Computing

While computers have been very useful in solving a great variety of problems, these computer solutions do not develop spontaneously from primordial elements. (At least, no one has witnessed such solutions spring into existence from nothing and lived to report the event.) Rather, computer solutions to problems depend upon the building of appropriate equipment (called **hardware**), the development of logical techniques (called **algorithms**) that specify how the problem can be solved, and the translation of these techniques into a form (called **software**) that can be utilized by the computers. Each of these aspects of problem solving requires considerable time and effort, and, unfortunately, each of them also has inherent limitations.

This chapter, therefore, reviews each of these major topics to provide an appropriate background for later discussions.

═══ PROBLEMS AND PROBLEM SOLVING ═══

To begin the discussion of the process involved in solving problems, consider a scenario that may describe a familiar pattern of events in a class.

- An instructor presents material (often in a dull lecture).

- Students are expected to read about concepts or techniques (this reading material may not be much more interesting than the lecture).

- Certain problems are assigned as homework.

- Students attempt to solve the problems given, perhaps using the techniques presented by the instructor or in the text.

- Problems may be clarified if students raise questions about the assignment.

While the tone of this scenario may not represent the ultimate in inspired education, the events do include many elements that are part of solving a very large number of problems. The order of events may vary somewhat from one situation to another, but problem solving in many scientific and technical settings involves work on the same basic issues. In the context of computing, problem solving frequently proceeds according to the following basic steps: *writing specifications, developing algorithms, design, coding algorithms, testing, and running programs,* and *maintaining programs.*

Writing Specifications. A **specification of a problem** is the careful statement of what problem is to be solved. In most mathematics, science, and engineering courses, this specification is complete in every assignment; students are told precisely what work is to be done. Unfortunately, however, even in a controlled classroom environment, it sometimes happens that the statement of a problem is flawed. For example, the statement may be ambiguous or contradictory. (Some faculty members have been known to state that an assignment actually has two parts: the first consists of determining what the question is supposed to be asking, and the second involves answering the corrected problem.)

In less controlled environments, the careful specification of a problem may take considerable work. For example, consider the traffic lights in a reasonably large city. Lights at each intersection may be red, amber, or green in each direction, and a timing device or controller changes the lights from one color to the next after a prescribed time interval. In this setting, a problem might be to develop a timing pattern for coordinating the lights, so that traffic flows most efficiently. Here the intuitive idea may seem clear— traffic should move smoothly from one place to another with little delay. However, making this idea precise may not be very simple. For example, how does one decide when traffic is moving smoothly? If most traffic is traveling out of town during the evening rush hour, say, how much should that traffic be delayed so that a single motorist can go in another direction? Is traffic delay measured as an overall average, or is there a maximum amount of delay that is acceptable at any intersection? Even if traffic does not seem to be badly congested, how would one know if another traffic light pattern would allow motorists to travel faster to their desired destinations? Any formal specification will need to address many questions of this type; otherwise it will be impossible to determine whether a proposed solution is satisfactory or not. Overall, specifications must indicate exactly what issues are to be addressed and how potential solutions will be evaluated.

Developing Algorithms. Once a problem is carefully specified, techniques or formulae can be developed to solve the problem. The careful statement of these appropriate techniques is called an **algorithm**. In an academic setting, such techniques are often discussed in class meetings or in course reading. Sometimes, a specific algorithm is even stated as part of the problem (e.g., "use Newton's Method to approximate $\sqrt{2}$ to three decimal places"). In a less structured setting, the choice of algorithm may be much less clear, and, in some cases, new algorithms may need to be discovered in order to solve a problem.

In evaluating a potential algorithm, clearly, one desirable characteristic is that the algorithm produces correct results. However, in many cases, such an algorithm still may not be acceptable. For example, one solution to the problem "Predict the Dow Jones Average for next Thursday" is "Wait until next Friday," but this approach may not be sufficiently timely. Similarly, one solution to the question "Find the call number of Walker's text *Introduction to Computing and Computer Science*" would be "Transport 100,000 people to the Library of Congress and have them search all of the shelves until the book is found." Such an approach would probably answer the question reasonably quickly, but it might use more resources than are reasonable. These examples suggest that algorithms must not only produce correct answers but also obtain those results in a timely manner using resources that are appropriate and available for the job.

Coding Algorithms. Once an algorithm is chosen, the use of computers typically requires that the algorithm be written in a form that a computer can interpret. Computers work by following instructions that they are given, and any algorithm must be translated into a form that uses only the special instructions that the computer can follow. The result of this coding is a **computer program**. (In the movie *2001*, the computer Hal responds to instructions given in English and to visual commands. Such understanding is commonly seen in movies. Realistically, however, computer understanding of natural language is still far from being realized, and the goal of much research in computer science is to be able to allow the automatic translation of speech or vision into a form that can be used by computers.) At a basic level, all information and instructions inside computers must be in a very primitive form, and considerable work is usually necessary to translate algorithms from English or another form understandable to people into a form a computer can interpret.

Testing and Running Programs. After an algorithm has been translated into a form a computer can use, one would hope that the program could be used to solve specific problems. Data from the specified problem could be entered into the computer, and the computer should produce the desired results. This step comprises the **running** of a program.

While the initial running of a program has been known to produce helpful and correct results, it is usually the case that some errors have occurred somewhere in the problem-solving process. Specifications may be incomplete or inaccurate, algorithms may contain flaws, or the coding processing may be incorrect. Edsger Dijkstra, a very distinguished computer scientist, has observed[1] that in most disciplines such difficulties are called *errors* or *mistakes*, but that in computing this terminology is usually softened, and flaws are called **bugs.** (It seems that people are often more willing to tolerate errors in computer programs than in other products, but more on this in later chapters.)

Unfortunately, many such errors or bugs arise frequently in many programs, particularly in large ones, and the next part of program development involves finding errors and correcting them. It can be very dangerous to rely on the output of a program until one is confident that the results are correct. Thus, programs are usually run with special data, the results of which are known ahead of time. This **testing** allows the results from a program to be compared with the previously known results to determine if errors are present. When such errors are found, it is necessary to find the cause of the error and to correct it, and this process is called **debugging.** When working on large projects, this process of testing and debugging can take considerable time and effort. Chapter 6 will demonstrate that, in many cases, it may be impossible to eliminate all errors from a program, even assuming that the specifications are perfectly written.

Maintaining Programs. At the beginning of this section, it was observed that, in giving assignments, an instructor sometimes will need to clarify or expand the statement of the problem. In addition (while it may be hard to believe), teachers have been known to change their minds about an assignment. In such cases, students may try to revise any work they have already done to meet the new specifications of the problem, but, if the problem has changed too much, the entire assignment may need to be done over.

This same situation arises commonly in working with complex problems that computers may help solve. For example, changes in tax laws or accounting procedures may require different calculations or records to be processed. Experience with a computer program may suggest ways the program might be changed to make it more useful. Errors (bugs) may be found that remained undetected during testing.

More generally, programs may need to be changed to accommodate new or changed circumstances or to correct errors. With short programs, such work can often be accomplished simply by rewriting the algorithm or code, but, in more complex settings, rewriting is simply too time-consuming and expensive. Thus, old programs are frequently reworked to meet the revised specifications, and this process is called **maintenance**. For large projects, this maintenance effort may extend for many years, and it may require a considerable investment in equipment, people, and time. In many cases, developers of programs will anticipate the need for maintenance, and algorithms and programming techniques will be used that may simplify the task. Throughout this maintenance activity, it is important to note that changes in one part of a program or the correction of some errors may introduce other errors. Thus, testing must continue throughout any maintenance work.

All of this discussion of problem solving has emphasized the specification of what a machine is to do. Such instructions comprise the **software** given to a computer. Computer software directs what steps a machine is to follow.

═══ **HARDWARE** ═══

All of the preceding discussion of problem solving and software would be rather meaningless, of course, without the existence of actual machines that can follow specified instructions in specified ways. This electrical or mechanical equipment forms the **hardware** of any computing system. Hardware includes one or more processors to execute instructions as well as devices to enter, store, retrieve, and display data.

In many ways, the development of hardware may follow much the same problem-solving process already described. To begin, it must be decided what a piece of hardware is to do, and specifications describing this job must be developed. Next, the electrical circuitry must be designed as the means to accomplish these specifications. This design phase must then move to actual production (which requires the physical layout of electrical components on chips or in machines), and manufacturing techniques must be developed and implemented. Finally, the concept of testing applies to hardware as much as it does to software.

While these steps suggest that there are many parallels in the consideration of hardware and software, there are also at least two important ways that hardware and software differ.

- Hardware is limited by the laws of physics and by the technology available to manufacture electrical and mechanical components. Software, on the other hand, works on the logical level of instructions in an environment that people can control. (After all, people build the computer upon which the software runs.)

- Hardware can wear out, while software cannot.[2] Most people, for example, have had the experience of riding in a car when something has gone wrong—a tire has gone flat, a water pump has given out (causing the car to overheat), gaskets have deteriorated (making oil leak). While these specific problems rarely occur in computers (e.g., few computers have tires), other physical or electrical difficulties are possible. Electrical components are susceptible to temperature fluctuations, power surges and outages, and electrical storms; the performance of physical devices may deteriorate due to wear. Machinery that once worked well may stop working or may produce different results due to electrical or mechanical failures. Such changes are not found in software, since the logical steps in an algorithm will not change. If an algorithm produces certain results at one time, then it will continue to produce those results whenever it is used.

The concept of maintenance for both hardware and software includes the

upgrading of capabilities. For hardware, however, the concept of maintenance also includes detecting the physical deterioration of a system. Anticipating such deterioration is often called **preventive maintenance**, a
process in which old components are serviced or replaced by new ones as
a way to prevent a machine from malfunctioning at a critical time. Such
preventive maintenance, however, is not a concern with software. (For
software, if a program is logically correct and has not been changed, then
it still must be logically correct.) Chapter 5 discusses some consequences
of maintenance and other issues related to hardware in more detail.

═══ OTHER ISSUES ═══

Beyond the topics of problem-solving techniques, software development,
and hardware, several other issues are closely related to the success of
using computers to help solve problems. The following notes outline two
additional factors. These topics are discussed in some depth in Chapters 8
and 9, respectively.

Human Factors. The use of most machinery (including computers) normally depends upon the assumption that people will use the equipment in
predictable ways. A machine's performance may suffer, however, if people
make mistakes or are not careful in using equipment. For example, several
movies have scenes in which thieves, relying upon high-performance automobiles to leave a burglary scene, are foiled when they accelerate in reverse
rather than in a forward gear. Campers may be ready to pitch a tent after
a day's hike, only to discover that they left the stakes (or the hammer to
drive the stakes) at home. Two children may be particularly proud of the
hairstyles they designed for each other, until they discover that they used
hair remover instead of shampoo. Throughout the history of computing,
similar and often outrageous errors have occurred when people have given
computers incorrect data to process and when incorrect procedures have
been followed.

Security. Good security is necessary for the integrity of many computer
applications. For example, businesses keep private financial records in
computer databases, colleges and universities store grade information, and
military installations house sensitive data about launching missiles and
deploying personnel and equipment. In such applications, tampering with
hardware, software, or data can have serious implications. Even with a
simple home computer, changing or erasing data can cause damage to documents or financial records that will take many hours of work to repair.
With this need for security, it may be important to ask how well a computer
system is protected against unauthorized or malicious tampering. (Even if

one knows that programs work correctly when they were constructed, how does one know they have not been changed?) Such issues can be difficult to answer for machines that are used by only one person and are isolated from other users and machines. These problems are compounded when several computers are linked together through cables or telephone lines, for then people or machines in one location may be able to read or change data stored in machines in different locations.

═══ SUMMARY ═══

1. Computing involves software (or instructions) running on specific hardware (or equipment).

2. The development of software requires several steps, including writing specifications, developing algorithms, coding algorithms, testing and running programs, and maintaining programs.

3. Both hardware and software may need to be upgraded as new demands are made or as errors in existing systems are found. In addition, hardware may wear out, so that preventive maintenance may be appropriate.

4. Beyond issues of hardware and software, the proper functioning of computer systems is complicated by the potential for human error in running equipment and by the need to protect hardware, software, and data from unauthorized, malicious, or inadvertent access or tampering.

═══ CONCLUSIONS AND IMPLICATIONS ═══

The use of computers requires the careful preparation of hardware and software. Since each of these areas is often quite complex, there is great potential for errors at every phase of the development process. This potential for error is heightened considerably by external factors, such as human error in entering data or running the system and deliberate or inadvertent access to or tampering with a computer system.

═══ DISCUSSION QUESTIONS ═══

1.1 While this chapter deals specifically with the role of computers within a problem-solving context, many of the points made here apply more broadly. Identify several problem-solving themes developed here for computing that apply in science and technology more generally.

1.2 Describe the role of computers in the problem-solving process.

    a. Much of this chapter is devoted to the process of solving problems with the help of a computer. How much of this process would still be required if a computer were not to be used?

    b. Computers require algorithms to be written in a specific language. Do you think this fact by itself can help the problem-solving process?

    Justify your answers.

1.3 The beginning of the chapter describes a common scenario involving events that may arise within a class setting. Relate each of these events to the problem-solving steps identified for computer solutions. For example, consider the following questions.

    a. In a class, how are specifications for problems determined?

    b. How does the statement, "Students attempt to solve the problems given, perhaps using techniques presented by the instructor or in the text," relate to the steps involving specifications, design, coding, testing, and maintenance?

    c. Describe the roles of the students, the instructor, and the book in determining algorithms.

    d. Where or how might maintenance be considered within a typical class?

1.4 Consider a problem that you recently encountered. If you have used computers recently, choose a problem for which the computer was part of the solution. Otherwise, choose a problem from a field of science, engineering, or mathematics (e.g., a physics, chemistry, mathematics, or computer science problem).

    a. How aware were you of the problem-solving process in approaching the problem?

    b. Relate the steps involved in specification, algorithm development, coding (if done as part of your solution), and testing.

    c. To what extent were you involved in each step?

1.5 What assumptions do you make about the reliability of the software that you use?

1.6 What would happen if you knew that the hardware upon which you were currently depending malfunctioned 10% of the time? Would you behave differently?

1.7 If you write programs, on which steps in the development of software do you generally spend the most time?

NOTES

1   Edsger Dijkstra, "On the Cruelty of Really Teaching Computing Science," *Communications of the ACM*, Volume 32, Number 12, December 1989, p. 1402.

2   Software involves only the instructions used to control computers, and it should not be confused with the physical disks that might be used to store the software. Certainly, disks can wear out, but the logical instructions cannot.

PART II
The Nature of Problems and Problem Solving

People use computers primarily because these machines can be helpful in solving problems. Chapter 1 stated that the first step of problem solving involves a careful identification of the actual problem to be solved. Specifications are needed to begin the problem-solving process. The task of developing specifications, however, often requires overcoming a wide range of difficulties, and the written specifications frequently differ from the actual problem of interest. Chapter 2 considers some of the factors that may hinder the writing of specifications, and such practical considerations form one type of limit on the effective use of computers.

After specifications are developed, the next step in the problem-solving process consists of identifying algorithms that will perform tasks required by the specifications. For this second phase to succeed, a problem must have two obvious properties.

1. The problem must have solutions. (If algorithms are not known, then they must be developed.)

2. Any algorithms chosen must be efficient enough to finish in an acceptable amount of time. (Algorithms that take centuries to complete the work are unlikely to be helpful, for example.)

While these points may be obvious, they raise questions that are far from trivial. Specifically, Property 1 suggests the question, *"Do all problems have solutions?"*, and Property 2 raises the question, *"If some algorithm exists for a problem, does it follow that the problem can be solved in a reasonable amount of time?"*

Unfortunately, the answers to each of these questions is *NO. Not all problems have solutions, and some problems with solutions cannot be solved in any reasonable amount of time.* Chapters 3 and 4 address each of these issues, respectively. In each case, the conclusions are not just theoretical, and some specific problems are identified that are unsolvable or that have no feasible solutions.

The Designer

The Government Inspector

The Mechanical Engineer

The Consumer

Stating Problems (What Is the Problem?)

T he goal of writing specifications is simply to give a statement of a problem in a clear, unambiguous, consistent, and complete way. Specifications identify the problem to be solved. They define *what* is to be done, while algorithms specify *how* to accomplish the task. In practice, the writing of specifications is complicated by at least five factors.

- While simple problems often have a clearly identified goal, more complex problems may initially depend upon only a vague vision of what is to be done. (For example, as noted in Chapter 1, a problem might start with the directive, "Develop a system to coordinate all traffic lights in a city.") When problems begin as poorly defined ideas, then much of the work of writing specifications is to clarify carefully what is meant.

- Writing in spoken languages like English can be ambiguous. These languages are not always sufficiently precise to yield statements that are clear and have only one interpretation.

- In writing solutions, people naturally base their work on their experience. As a result, many assumptions may not be mentioned, and established patterns of thought or action may not be reviewed.

- Different people may have different views of what is to be done. Further, in relatively complicated situations, even the same person may perceive a problem in several ways. As a result, specifications may not be consistent; different views of a problem may not logically agree with each other.

- It is easy to overlook something, particularly in complex situations. As a result, specifications may not be complete.

This chapter considers difficulties that arise from each of these factors and notes some ways that technology can be used to solve parts of these problems. The chapter concludes that it may be impossible to know if these difficulties have indeed been solved for a particular problem. Technology can help alleviate some troubles, but for complex problems there can never be a guarantee that all such difficulties are resolved. In practical terms, this places limits on the extent to which any computer system can be trusted to perform a task correctly.

$\equiv$ **ASSUMPTIONS** $\equiv$

Some difficulties in writing specifications are illustrated in the following exercise, taken from an elementary programming textbook.[1]

> Write a program that inputs an integer and then prints out the integer with commas inserted between every third integer. Thus, 123456789 should be printed 123,456,789 and -654321 should be printed -654,321.

In considering this problem, the great majority of students relate this problem to their experience of grouping digits in large numbers by hundreds, thousands, millions, etc. Thus, when printing 12345 or -1234567, these readers produce the output 12,345 and -1,234,567. A few students, however, group digits from left to right, producing 123,45 and -123,456,7. This alternate output violates some common assumptions or conventions about writing numbers, but the output does not violate the specifications actually given.

This example illustrates that the statement of a problem often relies upon additional background information that is not formally stated. People do not read and write specifications in isolation and removed from their experiences. Instead, people naturally bring their experiences and knowledge to bear whenever they work with language.

Unfortunately, computers do not share this common knowledge; computers "know" only the information they have been given. As a result, situations that people take for granted may be omitted when the computer processes data, unless appropriate data are supplied to the machine. As a simple example, one reasonably recent application of computing involved a type of program, called an expert system,[2] that was to diagnose certain illnesses and prescribe appropriate medications or therapy. Within this context, some symptoms naturally led to different conclusions for pregnant women than for other patients, so the program consistently asked patients if they were pregnant. While such questioning may seem quite reasonable, some male patients found it peculiar that they were asked if they were pregnant. This is a case in which common knowledge for people cannot be assumed when working with computers.

In another example, the F–16 fighter plane uses a computer to help control the raising and lowering of its landing gear, and the hardware and software have worked effectively in accomplishing this task. In an early version, however, the assumption was made that the plane would always be flying whenever the request was issued to raise the wheels. Unfortunately, violation of this unwritten assumption early in the testing of the plane caused significant damage. (Since that time, a new procedure, *weight-on-*

wheels, has been added to check this assumption, which is now formally specified.)[3]

These cases illustrate some of the difficulties that arise in identifying assumptions that underlie writing specifications. Some circumstances may seem so obvious that one never thinks about them. Frequently, these circumstances might be easy to describe, but, first, someone must realize that they should be included in the specifications. Identifying such assumptions may be particularly difficult in complex systems, since the written specifications for such situations often require hundreds or thousands of pages. Such documentation may describe many parts of a system, but details can get lost. Often, no one person really knows all the specifications, and specific pieces may fall into gaps between the responsibilities of different people.

═══ INCONSISTENCIES ═══

The earlier example concerning the insertion of commas within numbers illustrates different interpretations that are possible for the statement of a problem. That example also shows that a statement that seems completely clear and unambiguous to one person may not seem as clear to another. Alternatively, two people who find a statement to be unambiguous may have different interpretations of what is said. One type of inconsistency, therefore, can arise when two people read the same passage in different ways.

A second type of inconsistency may arise in large systems that are organized into parts. In such cases, decisions made for one part of the system may not be compatible with those made for another part. As an illustration, one large system was designed to record information about the inventory, orders, and billing for a company. Since each of these components were quite complex, the overall system was divided into several (five) pieces, each piece was designed separately, and the interactions among the various components were described in extreme detail. For example, when a customer placed an order, that information was entered into one component, which ran on one computer. These data were then sent to an inventory component, which organized shipping instructions and updated records. When the materials were shipped, information was sent back to the original ordering component. Subsequent communications linked the billing component system with the ordering information. In developing the specifications for this system, various types of transactions were described in great detail, flows of information were identified between various components of the system, and specific formats for messages were determined.

Trouble arose, however, when plans for handling errors in the various components were compared. For example, the inventory component assumed that, when it received a garbled message or request, the component that had sent the message would simply retransmit the request. The ordering component, however, logged each message it made, and retransmission implied that two separate requests required processing. Thus, the ordering component had no capability to retransmit messages. In this situation, each component had made decisions that seemed appropriate for that component, but the combination of these decisions created a significant problem for the overall system. As systems become more complex, this type of difficulty becomes increasingly likely, since more components must interact in increasingly sophisticated ways.

═══ OMISSIONS ═══

One of the hardest parts of writing specifications involves anticipating all possible circumstances that might occur. Users expect that a completed computer package will respond correctly to whatever input is presented. Similarly, when a computer is used to control machinery, it is often expected that the computer (and the machinery) will function appropriately in all circumstances. In practice, however, the computer will only follow procedures that it has been given, so the correct operation of a computer requires that designers plan for all possible situations.

Situations for Bicycle Riding. The difficulty of identifying all possible circumstances may be illustrated at a relatively simple level by considering what events one might need to anticipate when riding a bicycle. To be somewhat more specific, suppose that you are asked to identify the various situations that a cyclist should be prepared to handle. In considering this problem, some common occurrences may be easily identified. For example, bicyclists must anticipate vehicles passing in either direction, vehicles crossing at intersections, vehicles entering or leaving the road at driveways in the middle of a block, and crossing pedestrian traffic. Cyclists also must look ahead for potholes, deteriorated pavement, water drains, gravel, and soft shoulders. Such situations arise frequently when riding a bicycle, and the need to handle these events could be noted during a few weeks of observing cyclists.

Moving beyond normal operation, it is also relatively straightforward to anticipate various bicycle malfunctions that riders may need to handle. For example, common problems include flat tires (either due to blowouts or slow leaks), broken chains, chains that come off the pedal or wheel gears, inoperable gear shifts, and defective brakes.

In reviewing these lists, however, one may wonder whether any situations have been omitted; are these lists complete? (What do you think?) Unfortunately, the answer may depend upon whom is asked. For example, cyclists who ride regularly in a city know that urban riders must keep an eye out for people in parked cars who sometimes open car doors just as a bicycle approaches. Rural cyclists may note that special situations arise during high wind gusts. More generally, experiences in different settings may suggest a variety of additional circumstances, but these events may not be apparent to everyone.

Based on this discussion, it seems that several more circumstances should be added before the previous lists are complete. Even with such additions, however, it will still be difficult to know if the lists are complete. For example, the case about opening doors of parked cars still would not account for a situation once encountered by the author. The author was riding downhill along the right side of a main street (with cars parked next to the curb on the right) when a car passed the author on the left, stopped, and a passenger opened the car's right door immediately in front of the author's bike.

This example illustrates how it may be impossible to know when a list of circumstances is complete. The bicycle problem also illustrates two common, additional problems. First, the reviewers of existing specifications may not have sufficiently broad experience to consider some types of problems. For example, reviewers from the country might never note problems about parked cars, while city reviewers might not realize the significance of wind gusts or soft shoulders. Second, some situations may be so obvious that no one realizes that topics have been omitted. (The previous list of circumstances does not mention that brakes may deteriorate during rainstorms, for example. The effect of snow and ice is also not mentioned.) Overall, then, it may be rather easy to find issues that are omitted from specifications, but it is very difficult to know if specifications are complete.

Omissions in Real Systems. While the discussion of specifications for bicycle riding may be viewed as being somewhat hypothetical, the problem of omitted specifications is one that arises frequently in real systems. As shown in the following well-documented examples, the results can be startling:

- Control of the F–16 fighter plane is under the direction of a computer, so that the technologically advanced machine will be able to respond immediately to situations it encounters. In an early version of the plane, however, the navigation system did not distinguish between the northern hemisphere and the southern hemisphere, and the plane flipped over whenever it crossed the equator.[4]

- The United States maintains a Ballistic Missile Early Warning System to provide warnings of attacks by hostile powers. On October 5, 1960,[5] a computer interpreted echoes from several radar sensors as indicating that a massive attack had been launched on the United States by the

Soviet Union. In fact, the radar echoes indicated the rising moon, but no one had considered this possibility in writing specifications.

• In writing the guidance system for the Gemini V mission, no one realized the need to compensate for the motion of the Earth around the Sun. As a result, the splashdown missed its desired landing point by about 100 miles.[6]

With complex systems, it is virtually certain that some omissions will take place in writing specifications. As with anticipating possible situations for riding bicycles, it is not possible to know when all circumstances have been identified, and even seemingly obvious cases are often forgotten.

HANDLING DIFFICULTIES WRITING SPECIFICATIONS

The difficulties of assumptions, inconsistencies, and omissions in writing specifications have been present from the very beginning of computing. (Since similar difficulties arise in a range of scientific and engineering disciplines, one could even argue that these problems predate the introduction of computers by many years.) Given this history, it is hardly surprising that several approaches have evolved to address these problems, and these approaches comprise an important part of the field of software engineering. Some of the most widely used techniques involve an extensive reviewing process, careful selection of the language used to write the specifications, and computer-assisted software engineering (CASE) tools. As discussed in what follows, each of these techniques can have a significant impact on improving the writing of specifications. There is little hope, however, that all difficulties arising from unstated assumptions and omissions can ever be completely solved.

Reviews. In considering the identification of situations that arise while riding a bicycle, the earlier discussion in this chapter suggested that the initial lists of specifications can be expanded and refined if preliminary drafts are reviewed by a variety of experienced bicycle riders. This example illustrates two widely accepted principles.

1. Specifications must normally be developed iteratively in many stages. An initial draft may be prepared, but that draft provides only a starting point. This initial draft then is reviewed by several people, who suggest different ways to view the problem and who may try to identify assumptions, inconsistencies, and omissions. This feedback is used to develop a second draft. Reviewers next consider this new draft and provide further feedback. This process continues over a period of time: at each stage

that a new draft is written, the draft is reviewed, and feedback is used in preparing the next revision. Eventually, one expects some consensus to emerge. (One hopes that this agreement is achieved before a predefined schedule forces work to move ahead to the design phase.)

2. The development of specifications normally must involve the active participation of a variety of experts. In the bicycle example, many people may have ideas about cycling, but those who ride bicycles frequently can be expected to have the most insight. (At the other extreme, it is questionable how much help would be obtained from someone who rode a bicycle only as a child, 30 years ago.) Further, different experts may have varying experiences: cyclists who ride primarily in the city will encounter different situations than those who ride in rural areas. It is important, therefore, not only to ask experts but also to pick a group of them in which a range of perspectives is represented.

The process of reviewing by experts is complicated further in complex situations, which require a range of specialities. In planning a factory building, for example, architects have special training in design and materials; they know how buildings can be constructed, what techniques can be employed to achieve specific goals, and what costs might be associated with various approaches. Architects probably do not know, however, the detailed operation of the company that will move into the finished factory. Instead, the company's workers and management will know what machinery is needed, how it must be configured, how much space it needs, and what it requires for power, heat, air conditioning, water, etc. Details of maintenance and the normal flow of work from machine to machine also may be important in any final plan. In such circumstances, therefore, both architects and experienced factory workers should be involved in any reviewing process.

Language Selection. The need to consult experts with specialized knowledge has a considerable impact on the choice of language used to write specifications. Language selection often requires a compromise between two conflicting issues. First, as discussed earlier, English may invite ambiguities. Words often have several interpretable meanings, and pronouns or phrases may be interpreted as modifying several different objects. In an informal setting, many jokes and plays on words depend upon this potential for using words in many ways. For example, in the classic movie, *Mary Poppins*, one person asks, "Have you heard the story about the man with a wooden leg named Smith?" The second person replies, "What was the name of his other leg?"

Unfortunately, such difficulties arise frequently in other situations as well, where humor is not intended. For example, for many years, a traffic safety sign along the Ohio Turnpike proclaimed, "Drive slower when wet." While the sign probably did not mean that wet drivers should slow down, the sign never indicates what the word "wet" refers to. A similar difficulty with antecedents is found in an advertisement (which ran for several years on a small-town radio station) for a funeral home: "A granite marker can be a memorial and a tribute for *a life that was lived for generations to come*" (italics added). As these illustrations show, it is very easy for ambiguities to arise in natural language (e.g., English).

Since the goal of writing specifications is to avoid ambiguities and misunderstandings, the multiple meanings possible in English (or other natural language) can be particularly troublesome. This motivates the use of more formal language, such as mathematics or a programming language, in which all terms are precisely defined and in which words may be put together only in rather restricted ways. A mathematical proof, for example, uses language in a controlled way to present a logical argument. In such a proof, words and symbols are used in a formal notation system that states precisely what meaning is intended. Similarly, formal notation in chemistry provides an unambiguous way to specify the structure of molecules. Such formal systems of notation are developed specifically to allow a clear, precise, and unambiguous method of communication.

While such formal languages may avoid any possibility of ambiguity, such languages also have a disadvantage: some consulted experts often will not be comfortable using them. A factory worker or manager, for example, may not be accustomed to thinking in mathematical terms, and this could limit the effectiveness of any review that such a person might give. Further, many disciplines use a special jargon to express basic concepts, techniques, or objects, and experts in these disciplines think in this jargon. Thus, when they express their ideas about what specifications should say, experts will be most effective if they are allowed to use the language most familiar to them (which includes their specialized jargon).

In summary, natural languages, such as English, may be most familiar to experts trained in specialized areas, but such languages have a great potential for producing ambiguity and misunderstanding. Formal languages may resolve these difficulties, but they may require experts to become fluent in a new, previously unfamiliar language in which jargon from their field is excluded. Given such problems, the choice of an appropriate language for writing specifications can be extremely difficult.

CASE Tools. Many of the difficulties of writing specifications are particularly troublesome when trying to solve large or complex problems. Complicated problems often require consultations with experts in many fields, and the specifications typically extend to fill several volumes. Different parts of a problem may be viewed from several perspectives, and much of the challenge of developing specifications involves trying to manage the many facets of the problem.

One natural response to these difficulties involves the use of computers to manage the writing of complex specifications, just as it may be appropriate to use computers to help in finding the final solution to the problem. This view has motivated the development of a wide range of computer systems to aid in the creation of new software packages. At the simplest level, the computer can be used as a word processor, helping to store each draft of specifications and making editing particularly easy.

At more sophisticated levels, computer-assisted software engineering (CASE) tools can go well beyond mere word processing, and some CASE software attempts to integrate parts of the specification, algorithm design, and code generation phases of the problem-solving process. Several CASE packages, for example, allow the generation of specifications by focusing attention on the data to be stored and on how those data move from one step of processing to another. This gives rise to various levels of *data flow diagrams*, which are illustrated in Figure 2-1 which identifies the main steps that might be involved in processing everyday transactions for banking accounts. At this level, information for a transaction (account number, type of transaction [balance enquiry, withdrawal, deposit], and other data) is obtained. These data are used to update various files and records within the bank. Finally, any updates are placed in a log for audit purposes and the customer receives an acknowledgment of the transaction.

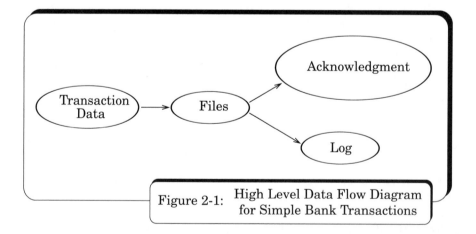

Figure 2-1:   High Level Data Flow Diagram for Simple Bank Transactions

Once such a high-level diagram is developed, CASE tools allow developers to focus on individual parts of the diagram. For example, various details must be considered concerning any transaction data that will be needed. In the jargon of some CASE packages, the "Transaction Data" node or process is "exploded" into more detailed "child" modules or processes that identify which data make up the "Transaction Data" and what relationships might exist among these data. At this more detailed level, specifics of each type of transaction might be identified. Thus, a balance enquiry may require only account number information, while a transfer may require the account number where money is to be withdrawn, the account to be credited, and the amount of the transfer. To be consistent with the high level diagram, all of this work within the "Transaction Data" node must yield a single output data record which can then be given to the "Files" node.

In supporting this specification and design work, CASE packages can help create easy-to-read diagrams at various levels, and these packages can check that the inputs and outputs at one level match those at a higher or lower level. While such checking can be done manually without the help of CASE tools, this consistency checking is extremely tedious for large, complex applications, and it is often impractical to perform manual checking at all levels of a large application.

Next, when information in a "Transaction Data" node requires information from a user, CASE tools can also help in the design of the format of information on a user's terminal. Here, CASE tools may allow the easy development of prototypes of input and output screens, so that designers can try several approaches for entering and presenting data. In some cases, once designers agree upon an appropriate format, CASE tools may be able to generate automatically code needed to run the desired interfaces. Thus, once a format is determined, no further programming may be needed to implement this interface in a program.

More generally, several CASE tools allow the integration of specification writing with the design phase. First, emphasis is placed upon the overall flow of data (data flow diagrams) or the logical organization of work into major subtasks (called *structure charts*). Next, each logical unit of data or each task is considered in greater detail, and constituent pieces of data or more detailed tasks are identified. At each stage, CASE tools allow the graphical or textual presentation of various levels of the work, and the tools may test the consistency of assumptions or conclusions at different levels. In this process, work proceeds by adding progressively more detail and structure until each element of a diagram or chart can be resolved completely and precisely. Eventually the process may evolve to a point where a complete algorithm has been specified to solve the problem at hand. In such situations, CASE tools sometimes allow the automatic translation of the resulting algorithm directly into code in a specified programming language. Sometimes, this code generation phase produces complete programs, but currently it seems more common for the CASE tools to generate elements of code that must be refined and assembled by skilled programmers.

Overall then, CASE tools may help the problem-solving process in several ways.

1. These tools may aid in the initial careful specification of a problem by providing an easy-to-use environment to identify needs. The resulting specifications may be displayed in graphical or textual ways, alternate views of the same specifications may be possible, and some consistency checking may be done automatically.

2. The design effort may be integrated with the development of specifications, starting with high-level views of data or tasks and then dividing complex data structures or tasks into more manageable pieces. This process of subdivision continues until each piece can be completely specified. At each stage, CASE tools may check that assumptions and capabilities identified at one level are consistent with those made at higher or lower levels.

3. Once the design process has progressed so that a complete algorithm has been developed, CASE tools may be able to translate some or all of the algorithm into parts of a computer program.

Through these capabilities, CASE tools allow specifications and designs to be viewed in various ways (e.g., using both graphics and text), and these tools may compare statements at various levels of detail. Each of these capabilities has important advantages.

- When specifications are presented in different forms, they can be considered by multiple reviewers from different perspectives. With different formats, reviewers may be more likely to identify assumptions and to discover omissions.

- Automated checking can test for internal consistency, so that statements made at one level agree with those at other levels. Automated checking also can identify some common errors (e.g., processes that require various pieces of data as input but which do not produce output of any type).

- CASE tools can make software developers more efficient by integrating several development phases and by helping in the generation of finished programs.

On the other hand, CASE tools cannot resolve all difficulties surrounding the production of software. For example, assumptions must be made in developing the tools themselves, and tools that work in one context may not apply to other types of applications. Omissions can be detected only when some evidence demonstrates that additional information is needed.

Internal inconsistencies may be discovered, but inconsistencies with external circumstances or data are more difficult to identify. CASE tools may help reduce errors and increase efficiency in developing specifications and algorithms, but people still must solve each step of the development process and people must decide when specifications and algorithms meet perceived needs. Unfortunately, since subjectivity is involved in some of these human elements, CASE tools can play only a limited role in some situations. In many cases, there simply is no way of knowing when one has stated all of one's assumptions explicitly and taken all possibilities into account.

SUMMARY

1. The first stage of the problem-solving process requires identifying the problem through the writing of clear, unambiguous, consistent, and complete specifications.

2. Fundamental difficulties arise in writing specifications, due to complications arising from assumptions, inconsistencies, and omissions.

3. Reviews, choice of languages, and CASE tools can help reduce errors, inconsistencies, and omissions. Even with these techniques, however, serious troubles (due to assumptions or omissions in specifications) still plague a wide range of working systems.

4. Even with the ever-expanding power and sophistication of CASE tools and other software development techniques, there is no evidence to suggest that future systems will be completely free of the types of errors discussed in this chapter. Advanced techniques may reduce errors, but specifications can still be expected to contain oversights and mistakes.

CONCLUSIONS AND IMPLICATIONS

This chapter argues that for complex problems it is simply not possible to develop specifications that are guaranteed to be free of unstated assumptions, inconsistencies, and omissions. In other words, in developing software, one must work under the assumption that the specifications contain mistakes. Some mistakes may be trivial, others may be very serious. Due to the limitations inherent in developing specifications, however, the seriousness of the errors cannot even be predicted.

As a result, systems used to solve complex problems must be built in ways that accommodate these errors. This suggests two important properties of such systems. First, systems should be constructed to minimize the impact that errors might have. (Such systems are sometimes said to be *fault-tolerant*.) Second, systems must be provided with the capacity to repair errors when they do arise. One must not assume that certain situations cannot arise, since errors in specifications (and in algorithms and code) are always possible.

═══ DISCUSSION QUESTIONS ═══

2.1 This chapter opens with a cartoon giving different perspectives concerning a swing. Discuss how these perspectives illustrate various difficulties of writing specifications, as discussed in this chapter.

2.2 Software vendors are continually developing and expanding various CASE tools that can help in writing and refining specifications. Read some recent articles on particular CASE tools to determine what they do, how they may be used, and how they aid the software development process.

2.3 Consider a request by an instructor to a college registrar which states, "Please send me a list of those students who are failing at midterm." What is ambiguous about this request? Point out assumptions, inconsistencies, and omissions in the statement. Rewrite the problem statement unambiguously. Show it to a friend or colleague and ask for criticisms.

2.4 Discuss a system that you currently use.

   a. What are your assumptions about its specifications? (For example, for a word processor, how long a document could you handle? What percent of the dictionary is in the spelling checker?)

   b. How do you rely upon those specifications and what might be some consequences of misunderstanding those specifications?

2.5 Many jokes are based on misunderstanding specifications. For example, the Amelia Bedelia series of children's books are based on such misunderstandings. Find several examples of these and restate the ambiguities that caused the problems.

NOTES

1 Henry M. Walker, *Problems for Computer Solutions Using BASIC*, Winthrop Publishers Inc, Cambridge, Massachusetts, 1980, Section 4.3, Exercise 19, p. 115.

2 While expert systems are described in somewhat more detail in Chapter 8, these programs simply provide a relatively new way of specifying instructions to a computer. The details of the software are rather different when comparing expert systems with more traditional programs, but the need for logically and unambiguously specifying information is the same.

3 Other problems with the F–16 are reported in *Software Engineering Notes,* October 1986, p. 6.

4 Reported in a letter by Earl Boebert in *Software Engineering Notes*, Volume 5, Number 2, April 1980, p. 5.

5 See, for example, "Moon Stirs Scare of Missile Attack," *New York Times*, 8 December 1960, pp. 71–72.

6 See J. Fox, *Software and Its Development,* Prentice-Hall, Englewood Cliffs, New Jersey, 1982, pp. 187–188.

An outlander and his wife driving along stopped and asked an old-timer how to get to Millinocket.

He scratched his head and said, "Well, you turn 'round and go 'till you git to Ed Brown's silo. Take a left there and go 'bout five miles 'til you git to a red barn. Take a right there and go another three miles 'till you come to a cemetery. Take a left at the cemetery ... now, lemme see! Go straight there for – no! Gol darn it, you can't get there from here."

—From *Maine Sampler,* a Collection of Maine Humor by Bill Sawyer. Published by Down East Books, Camden, Maine, 1986.

Unsolvability

O nce specifications are determined for a problem (e.g., how to get to Millinocket), the design phase starts. Algorithms must be identified or developed to solve the problem (e.g., one must stop to ask directions).

In many areas of life, people have come to expect that such answers exist (e.g., people know it is possible to get to Millinocket). Similarly, in technical fields, the many visible successes of science support the viewpoint that answers can be found to many (perhaps all) problems. Of course, science has not solved all problems yet, but it is not uncommon to meet people who believe that solutions can always be found, given enough effort (and time and money). With this rich history of technological success, it is reasonably uncommon to hear the question, *Do all technical questions have solutions?*

The purpose of this chapter is to consider this question and to conclude that solutions are not always possible. Sometimes one must conclude, *no! Gol darn it, you can't get there from here.* Further, the discussion that leads to this conclusion is not purely theoretical. The chapter describes one particularly simple problem from computer science that has no solution. Analogous problems from other scientific disciplines are also noted. Thus, not only can one speculate that some problems exist that are not solvable; one can identify specific problems that are known to have no solution.

═══ THE HALTING PROBLEM ═══

One of the simplest problems known to be unsolvable is called the *Halting Problem*. In what follows, this problem is described and then a proof is outlined to show that the problem cannot be solved. This suggests some conclusions.

The basic idea of the Halting Problem depends upon the notion of a loop in programming. One of the reasons that computers are so powerful is that once they are given instructions to perform a task they can be told to repeat that task over and over again. For example, part of a program to control the traffic lights for one street at an intersection might have the following outline:

```
Initially
   1. The green light is on
   2. The red and amber lights are off
Continue forever Steps 3 - 8
   3. Turn on the amber light; turn off the green light
   4. Wait 20 seconds
   5. Turn on the red light; turn off the green light
   6. Wait 40 seconds
   7. Turn on the green light; turn off the red light
   8. Wait 40 seconds
```

Here, after an initial setup, the same six steps are repeated at length. (A more complete outline would involve the lights for cross streets and possibly pedestrian lights, but the same pattern of repetition would be similar.) In programming, such a repetition of steps is called a **loop.**

In some cases, the problem demands that a loop continue without end, and such a loop is said to be **infinite.** In other cases, a loop is needed to repeat some instructions for a certain amount of time and then stop. For example, part of a program to print a table for converting quarts to liters might have the following outline:

```
Repeat Steps 1 - 3 with Quarts being 1, 2, 3, ... , 20.
   1. Compute Liters corresponding to Quarts
          by the formula:  Liters = Quarts / 1.056710
   2. Print the values of Quarts and Liters
          in two columns on the same line
   3. Move to a new line
```

Given this outline, the resulting table will contain 20 lines, each line listing a quart value and its metric equivalent in liters. In this application, a loop allows the same instructions to be repeated for 20 values of quarts, and this makes the instructions concise. To make this program more helpful, one might ask a user to specify what range of values is desired in the table. For example, the user might specify the range 20 to 30 quarts instead of requiring the computer to print the same table each time the program is run. In such a case, the resulting program would still have a loop, but the number of lines in the resulting table would depend upon what the person running the program requested.

These examples highlight two important characteristics of algorithms and computer programs.

• Algorithms and programs may contain loops, and these loops may be infinite or finite.

• The amount of work done in an algorithm or program may depend upon what data are typed by an individual user of the program.

As algorithms and programs become more complex, it may not be obvious whether or not the computations will eventually stop. Some loops may be clearly finite, but, for others, the results may depend upon various computations that the program may make. (For example, if a program keeps track of the winnings or losses of a gambler, the program may be told to keep going until the gambler wins over $1,000. Depending upon luck, the gambler may never win this amount, so the program might continue forever.)

This fact gives rise to the **Halting Problem:**

> Given a program and an input to the program, determine if the program
> will eventually stop when it is given that input.

Since loops are a fundamental part of virtually all algorithms and programs, an answer to this problem would be particularly helpful in many applications. The value of this answer is enhanced further by the fact that some programs contain errors, that may cause loops to be infinite when that is not the desired result. (For example, a relatively common error involves omitting one or more steps in a loop. If one is not careful, this can give rise to an infinite loop that contains a single instruction; it tells a printer to go to the next page. In the early days of computing, before safeguards were introduced to protect against this specific error, the result could be an arc of computer paper leaving a printer at a high rate of speed and forming a large pile near one wall of the room.)

In trying to answer the Halting Problem, one approach is to start the algorithm or program with the given input and wait to see what happens. If processing stops, then the result is clear; the program cannot be stuck in an infinite loop. However, if the program does not stop in a reasonable amount of time, then the answer to the Halting Problem is not so clear. It is possible that the program just needs more time to finish; the program may stop, but one needs to wait longer. It is also possible, however, that the program will never stop. Unfortunately, on a practical level, it is not possible to distinguish between a program that is caught in an infinite loop and one that is still working, so the "try it, wait and see" approach cannot be relied upon to answer the Halting Problem.

Unfortunately, the following discussion shows that no other approach can be found to solve this problem either.

Proof That the Halting Problem Is Unsolvable.[1] A simple approach
to showing that a problem cannot be solved would be to consider all of the
possible solutions to the problem and then to show that each one contains
a flaw. If every proposed solution is incorrect in some way, then no solution
exists.

At first glance, this simple approach may seem outrageously naive, since
it may seem hopeless to list all possible solutions to the Halting Problem (or
to any other problem). However, this approach is precisely the basic idea
of an ingenious proof, first found by Alan Turing in 1936, that the Halting
Problem cannot be solved. In this proof, one starts with any proposed
solution to the Halting Problem and then one shows that that solution must
be flawed. Then, since any solution must be incorrect, one much conclude
that no solutions exist.

To begin the proof, then, suppose you are given a proposed solution to the
Halting Problem. To be more precise, suppose you are given a computer
program (or algorithm) A that has two inputs, a computer program P and
some input I for that program P. When P and I are entered into A, then A
indicates whether P will halt or not when it is given input I. All programs P
and inputs I are allowed as data for A, and in each case A will determine if
the program entered will halt with the given input. To be concrete, suppose
that A prints "H" (for *Halt*) if a given program halts with the given input,
and suppose that A prints "L" (for *Infinite Loop*) if the given program does
not halt. Schematically, the workings of program A are shown in Figure
3-1.

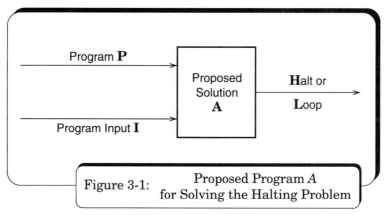

Figure 3-1:   Proposed Program A
for Solving the Halting Problem

Given this proposed solution A, the proof that A is flawed proceeds with
three steps or observations.

1. Some observations on coding algorithms.

2. Using A to construct a new program N.

3. Proof that A fails to give a correct response for N, showing that the proposed algorithm A is incorrect.

While each of these steps requires some care in the context of a formal proof, the ideas behind them are relatively straightforward. The following discussion gives these ideas, omitting some technical details.

Observations on Coding Algorithms.
In specifying an algorithm for a computing application, one customary step requires that the algorithm be written in a form that a computer can interpret. At a formal level, this means that it must be possible to translate an algorithm into a formal language, such as a programming language.

However, a computer can interpret the symbols in a language either as a program or as data. A computer does not distinguish between words in a program and characters or numbers used as data. A machine cannot determine if a specific piece of data is a character or a number.

Therefore, once an algorithm is written in a formal computer language, the resulting text may be considered either as the original program or as data. Further, when considered as data, this information can be used as input to programs.

Given this observation, it is possible to run a program using a copy of itself as data. Schematically, this approach is shown in Figure 3-2 for a program P.

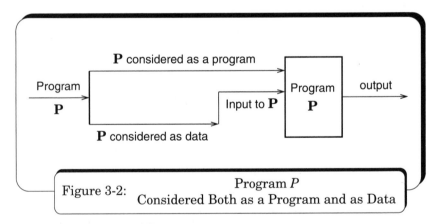

Figure 3-2:   Program P Considered Both as a Program and as Data

Using Proposed Algorithm A to Construct a New Program N.
The proposed solution A to the Halting Problem is supposed to take program P and data input I as inputs and then determine whether P eventually stops when given I as input. As a special case, therefore, algorithm A must be able to determine whether any program P halts when it is given a copy of itself as input.

Said differently, using the preceeding observations, any program P may be viewed either as a program or as data. Thus, given a program P, it is reasonable to ask whether P will eventually stop processing when it is given P as input. Since algorithm A is designed to answer such questions, one should be able to give A any program P as a program and another copy of P as data and then receive a response indicating whether P halts with P as input. This response can then be used to construct a new algorithm (or program) N (for *New*).

Algorithm N will be a new algorithm that takes program P as input. In its processing, algorithm N uses the proposed algorithm A as follows:

Outline for Algorithm N

```
1. Read a program P
2. Use Algorithm A to determine if P halts
          when given P as input
3. If Algorithm A indicates P halts with P as input
        then enter an infinite loop
              (e.g., add 1 + 1 forever)
    If Algorithm A indicates P never halts with input P
        then print the word "DONE" and stop
```

Schematically, the new algorithm N takes program P as input and either prints "Done" or continues processing forever, as shown in Figure 3-3.

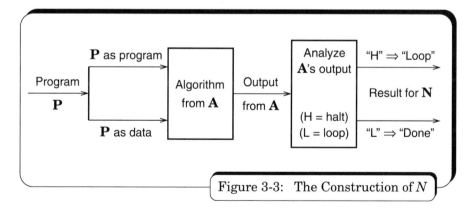

Figure 3-3: The Construction of N

With this outline, the new program N will take programs as input and then either go into an infinite loop or stop by printing the word "Done.". Because of its construction, N will loop for some inputs and stop for others.

Proof That the Proposed Algorithm A Is Incorrect. Since N is a program that will stop at some times and not stop at others, the proposed algorithm A should be able to determine when N will stop and when it will proceed into an infinite loop. Certainly, if A is a correct algorithm, it must be able to work for N as well as for any other programs.

Now, consider what happens when A is applied to this new program, N using input data N. If A specifies that N will terminate, then the construction of N specifies that N will go into an infinite loop. On the other hand, if A determines that N will not terminate, then N is constructed so that it will stop by printing the word "Done." In either case, algorithm A will have given the wrong answer as to whether program N terminates when given data N. Thus, the proposed algorithm A does not work in all cases.

Conclusions about the Halting Problem. The argument just completed indicates that any proposed solution to the Halting Problem cannot work in all cases; *any proposed solution must be flawed.*

In reviewing this argument, it is crucial to note that this conclusion does not depend upon what solution might be suggested for the Halting Problem. The conclusion applies to all solutions that have already been proposed and to any other approaches that one might develop in the future. The conclusion will not be changed by taking more time or by being more clever in trying to solve the problem. There simply is no possible algorithm that solves the Halting Problem. The phraseology of the story at the beginning of this chapter applies to the effort to solve the Halting Problem: "Gol darn it, you can't get there from here."

More generally, this consideration of the Halting Problem demonstrates one frustrating and unsettling conclusion about computing in particular and about technology in general. Some problems simply cannot be solved by technology, regardless of how much work is expended and how many resources are devoted to the attempt. There are some fundamental limits to what computers (and technology) can do.

═══ ANALOG ═══

While the previous discussion shows that the Halting Problem cannot be solved, it is worthwhile to note that similar situations arise in other branches of mathematics and science. The Halting Problem is only one in a family of problems that cannot be resolved by technology. For example, two analogous situations arise in physics and in mathematics. The following paragraphs describe these situations briefly.

Heisenberg's Principle of Uncertainty. In physics, it is common to ask questions about where objects are located and how fast and in what direction they are going. A typical physics problem asks, "Find the position and velocity of a given particle." On a large scale, such questions are answered routinely. For example, the position and velocity of a rocket are measured constantly during a space flight.

On a very small scale, however, answering such a question is more difficult. Specifically, consider an electron within a particular atom. Following the particle model of the electron, one thinks of the electron as a particle, and it is appropriate to consider where it is and how fast it moves in what direction. Physicists talk about the position and velocity of electrons, but, on a practical level, one might ask just how this position and velocity could be measured.

In order to measure position and velocity, some energy (such as light or a magnetic field) will be expended. The electron's movement will affect some instruments, and changes in those instruments will allow an observer to compute position and velocity. Unfortunately, given the energy levels in question, instruments will also have some effect upon the electron itself. The interaction of the electron with the light or the field used to observe it will affect both the instrumentation and the electron itself. This fundamental observation forms the basis for Heisenberg's Principle of Uncertainty, which in physics states that one cannot know both the position and the velocity of an electron at the same time. Estimates may be possible, but it is not possible to know exactly both where an electron is and how it is moving.

As with the Halting Problem, Heisenberg's Principle of Uncertainty states that there are some things that people cannot know. Science can be successful in many ways, but some specific problems cannot be solved.

Russell's Paradox. A statement of a similar problem is known in mathematics as Russell's Paradox, which concerns whether it is possible to construct some sets. Specifically, the paradox asks whether there can be a set of all sets, and the conclusion is that such a construction is impossible. While the argument involves some technical results from set theory, the same ideas form the basis of the following story,[2] which was originally proposed by Bertrand Russell himself.

> A barber in Seville places the following sign in his window.
>
> I shave all those men in town, and only those men, who do not shave themselves.
>
> Using the information from the sign, who shaves the barber?
>
> If he shaves himself, then he belongs to the set of men who shave themselves. But his sign says he never shaves anyone in the set. Therefore, he cannot shave himself.

> If someone else shaves the barber, then he is a man who does not shave himself. But the sign says he does shave all such men. Therefore, no one else can shave the barber.
>
> Thus, no one can shave the barber.

One explanation of this story suggests that the barber never shaves (and thus has a long beard). Alternately, one might argue that the barber is not male. However, if one follows traditional assumptions from Russell's time (1903), then neither of these explanations is adequate, and the sign in the window yields a paradox. There is no satisfactory answer to the question.

Such paradoxes comprise the basis for a wide range of popular books and amusements.

═══ SUMMARY ═══

1. The Halting Problem asks one to find an algorithm that will determine whether or not programs will halt for various inputs.

2. While a solution to the Halting Problem would be particularly helpful in many applications, Turing showed that the Problem has no solutions. It is impossible to find a correct solution to the Halting Problem.

3. The inability to solve the Halting Problem has parallels in other disciplines. Russell's Paradox from mathematics illustrates another type of problem that has no solution. Similarly, Heisenberg's Principle of Uncertainty from physics identifies another context where answers cannot be known.

═══ CONCLUSIONS AND IMPLICATIONS ═══

While technology in general and computing in particular have been extraordinarily successful in solving a wide range of problems, there are some problems that cannot be solved by using technology. Further, these difficulties cannot be corrected by spending more time, money, or resources on the problems or by being more clever.

In such cases, problems can be addressed only by looking outside of the technical world. For example, political or social policies might be used to resolve global conflicts by eliminating the need for the technology in the first place. (If nuclear weapons were eliminated, for instance, there would be no need for a technological solution to control them.)

Although technology can be successful in dealing with many issues, it does have limitations. Technology cannot even determine whether a program will become caught in an infinite loop.

═══ DISCUSSION QUESTIONS ═══

3.1 This chapter indicates that some problems are solvable and some are not.

    a. Define what the term *solvable* means in a problem-solving context.

    b. What does it mean to say that "you solved a problem"?

3.2 Consider some data processing examples that contain loops. For example, a money machine is continuously being sampled to determine if there are requests for service. Cite other examples where infinite loops are desirable.

3.3 Find some examples in disciplines other than physics that use Heisenberg's Uncertainty Principle as a model to describe why some questions are unanswerable. Do you believe that this is an excuse to avoid confronting difficult problems? Would an approach based on a rigorous proof approach aid in solving the problem? Explain your answer.

3.4 Find examples of problems for which you believe there are no solutions. Why do you believe these problems are unsolvable? What would it take for someone to convince you that a solution exists?

NOTES

1   The details of the proof on the next few pages involve considerable thought and sophistication, and this material may seem much more difficult than other discussions in this book. While these details are interesting and important, they are not as important to what follows as the conclusion that the Halting Problem is unsolvable. For this reason, at first reading, you may wish to skim the next few pages. A more extensive discussion of the Halting Problem may be found in most texts that discuss the theory of computation or automata theory. Some references appear in the short, annotated bibliography at the end of this book.

2   Martin Gardner, *aha! Gotcha*, W. H. Freeman and Company, San Francisco, California, 1982, p. 16.

CHAPTER 4

"How far is it to Kennebunkport?"
"'Bout 26,000 miles, the way you're going."

> —From *Maine Sampler,* a Collection of Maine Humor by Bill Sawyer. Published by Down East Books, Camden, Maine, 1986.

Nonfeasibility

Chapter 3 showed that some problems cannot be solved; this chapter considers situations where solutions exist, but they all require too much time or too many resources to be feasible. In getting to Kennebunkport, there may be many ways to proceed, and some routes may be more efficient that others. Sometimes, however, feasible solutions may not exist.

The feasibility of solutions often depends upon how much work must be done and how many resources are required to do this work. While the analysis of solutions can produce worthwhile information, sometimes it is easy to be fooled by the resulting numbers. The following abbreviated fable illustrates one type of problem.

A FABLE: A KING MEETS THE COMBINATORIAL EXPLOSION

Once upon a time, a king needed a great task performed. In response, a clever young man named Paul agreed to do the work, if the amount of payment was adequate. When the king asked Paul about his requirements for compensation, Paul responded that the king might choose between two options:

Option 1. Payment could consist of one fifth of the crops produced in the kingdom for each of the following five years, or

Option 2. Payment could be made as follows:

- One kernel of corn would be given for the first square of a chess board.

- Two kernels of corn would be paid for the second square.

- Four kernels (twice the previous amount) would be paid for the third square.

- Eight kernels (again twice the previous) would be paid for the fourth square.

- This counting would continue, with successive doubling for each square, until payment was made for each square of a chess board.

When the king considered these choices, the first option seemed justified for the great service required, but the king liked the sound of the second option better. After all, the king reasoned, how could a few kernels of corn compare with a fifth of the crops harvested for five years – Option 1 would give a full year's crops over a five year period. With this, the king contracted with Paul for the work using Option 2 as the form of payment.

A year went by, Paul completed the work, and it was time for payment. The king ordered baskets of grain to be brought, and the process was begun of counting kernels of corn. For the first row of the chess board (eight squares), the payment involved $1 + 2 + 2^2 + 2^3 + 2^4 + 2^5 + 2^6 + 2^7$ or $1 + 2 + 4 + 8 + 16 + 32 + 64 + 128 = 255$ kernels of corn, much less than a bushel.[1]

For the next row, the payment was

$$2^8 + 2^9 + 2^{10} + 2^{11} + 2^{12} + 2^{13} + 2^{14} + 2^{15}$$

or 65,280 corn kernels. Since a bushel of corn typically contains about 72,800 kernels,[1] this payment was still less than a bushel of corn.

With the next row, however, the king became uneasy. The payment for this row was

$$2^{16} + 2^{17} + 2^{18} + 2^{19} + 2^{20} + 2^{21} + 2^{22} + 2^{23}$$

or 963,040 corn kernels, which is about $13\frac{1}{4}$ bushels. While this amount still was relatively small, the numbers were getting larger, and only three of the eight rows of the board had been considered.

During the counting for the next row, the king thought ahead to the last (64th) square. Following the pattern he now understood, this last square alone would cost 2^{63} kernels of corn – roughly 8×10^{18} kernels or about 110,000 billion bushels! Certainly, such an obligation could never be met.[2] With such a staggering debt, the king abdicated his throne, and the mathematically sophisticated Paul became monarch of the kingdom.

═══ COMBINATORIAL EXPLOSION ═══

In this fable, a plan for payment was chosen that could never practically be completed. Similar difficulties arise in many situations where computers are used as part of a proposed solution to a problem. In computing applications, however, it is often hard to appreciate the amount of work or the number of resources required to do a task, since computers seem to work at such tremendous speeds and they can store such vast amounts of data. For example, it can be hard to comprehend the significance of such measures as a million (10^6) instructions per second (MIPS) or storage for 10^9 characters (a gigabyte).

Payments in Corn. In reviewing the fable, it is instructive to note that the key to the huge payments involved the doubling of the kernels of corn for each square. If, instead, the number of kernels was increased by 2 for each square, then the payments would have been much more modest.

- Square 1 requires 1 kernel.
- Square 2 requires 3 kernels.
- Square 3 requires 5 kernels.
- Square 4 requires 7 kernels.
  $\vdots$
- Square i requires $2i - 1$ kernels
  $\vdots$
- Square 64 requires 127 kernels.

Overall, this amounts to $1 + 3 + 5 + \ldots + 127 = 4{,}096$ kernels of corn (about 0.056 bushels). Such an amount is quite small indeed. The difficulty with the payment in the fable, therefore, is not that the payment increased for each square; rather the huge numbers came about because payments doubled.

For future reference, it can be enlightening to determine the effect of other payment schemes on the overall size of payments. For example, one might ask what would happen if payments depended upon a power of the number of squares considered. For example, suppose the number of kernels was determined as the second power (the square) of the number of the board square considered. In this case, the payments would proceed as follows:

- Square 1 requires $1^2 = 1$ kernel.
- Square 2 requires $2^2 = 4$ kernels.
- Square 3 requires $3^2 = 9$ kernels.
- Square 4 requires $4^2 = 16$ kernels.
  $\vdots$
- Square i requires i^2 kernels
  $\vdots$
- Square 64 requires $64^2 = 4{,}096$ kernels.

Here, the payments are increasing considerably faster than when they increase by only two for each square, but the total $(1 + 4 + 9 + 16 + \ldots + 4{,}096 = 89{,}440$ kernels (about 1.2 bushels) is still manageable.

While these alternate formulae seem to yield significantly smaller payments of corn for Paul, other formulae can give much bigger results. For example,

1. Start with 1 kernel for square 1.
   - For square 2, multiply the amount from square 1 by 2.
   - For square 3, multiply the amount from square 2 by 3.
   - For square 4, multiply the amount from square 3 by 4.

$$\vdots$$

- For square i, multiply the amount from square $i - 1$ by i.
  Note: Here, one can show that the payment for square i is $i \times (i-1) \times (i-2) \times \ldots 2 \times 1$. This number is sometimes called **i factorial** and is written $i!$.

2. For square 1, pay 1^1 kernels.
   - For square 2, pay 2^2 kernels.
   - For square 3, pay 3^3 kernels.

   $$\vdots$$

   - For square i, pay i^i kernels.

Each of these formulae produces much bigger payments than were required of the king. (The reader may find it interesting to determine the size of the payments due in each case for the first row of squares on a chess board.)

In addition to the formula used for successive squares, one might ask the effect of taking different sizes of chess boards. For example, suppose a board had 20 or 50 or 100 squares. These computations are left as an exercise.

While it may seem a bit corny to consider such kernels in a textbook about computing, similar issues arise in analyzing various solutions to problems. For example, suppose a computer is to process some data. Normally the amount of work involved will depend both upon the particular approach that is taken to solve the problem and upon how many data are present.

A Sorting Example.[3] To be more specific, consider the task of placing n pieces of data in order – perhaps names of people are to be printed in alphabetical order or mailing lists are to be prepared in zip-code order. Since this task, called **sorting**, is very common, many efficient approaches have been devised to perform the job. While some of the fastest solutions are quite complex, two rather simple (but nonoptimal) approaches are sufficient to illustrate the points of interest here.

1. *A Selection Sort*
   - Go through all n pieces of data and select the largest.
   - Go through the remaining pieces of data to find the largest remaining.

   $$\vdots$$

   - After selecting the i biggest pieces of data, go through the remaining $n - i$ pieces of data and select the largest.

   $$\vdots$$

   - This process is continued until all data are processed.

2. *Exhaustive Listing and Search*
   - In this approach, all possible arrangements or permutations of the data are generated until a sorted one is found.
   - In the Prolog programming language, such an algorithm may be specified as:

$$SORT(InitialData, \ FinalData) : -$$
$$Permutation(InitialData, \ FinalData),$$
$$Ordered(FinalData).$$

The following analysis clarifies some fundamental differences between these approaches. For the Selection Sort, a main step is required for the selection of each piece of data. Since there are n items altogether, this indicates that there must be n major steps in the execution of this sorting algorithm. Within each step, all data items remaining must be reviewed to find the largest. This yields the following conclusions.

At step 1, all n items must be reviewed – if the review of one number requires one unit of work, then this step would require about n units of work to complete.

For step 2, $n-1$ data items must be reviewed. Again if each item can be reviewed with one unit of work, then this step may be performed in $n - 1$ units of work.

$$\vdots$$

For step i, $i-1$ data items were selected previously, so $n-i+1$ items remain. As before, this would require $n-i+1$ units of work.

Overall, then, this approach to sorting requires

$$(n) + (n-1) + (n-2) + \dots + 2 + 1$$

units of work. Using algebra, one can show that this is the same as $n(n+1)/2$ work units.

In contrast, the work required for the Exhaustive Listing and Search will depend upon how permutations of data are generated. If one is lucky, a sorted permutation of the data will be considered very early. However, if one is not lucky, the desired sorted permutation may not be found until all other possibilities have been considered. Here, work may require both the generating of new permutations of data and the checking of whether the permutation is sorted. If one unit of work is considered to involve both the generation of a new permutation and the checking of whether it is ordered, then the total work required will depend upon how many permutations are reviewed before a sorted one is found. In the worst case, one might have to consider all possible permutations of the n pieces of data, and one can show that $n \times (n-1) \times (n-2) \times \ldots \times 2 \times 1 = n!$ permutations are possible. Thus, altogether it is possible that $n!$ units of work may be required.

Following this analysis of these two approaches, it is now possible to make a rough comparison of how efficient they might be. The Selection Sort approach required about $n(n+1)/2$ review units of work while the Exhaustive Search approach required $n!$ generation units of work. Since "review units" may not be the same as "generation units," exact comparisons are not possible. (There may also be differences in the way these steps are done on different machines.) However, Figure 4-1 still provides a means to reach some conclusions. For example, for 10 data items, the selection approach requires $10 \times 11/2$ or 55 steps, while the exhaustive search approach requires 10! or 1,612,80 steps. Clearly the selection approach is faster, since the roughly n^2 steps for selection require substantially less work than the $n!$ steps required for the other approach. In a practical test of these approaches conducted by the author, the Selection Sort processed 9 or 10 data items in well under a second, while the Exhaustive Listing and Search took 1 minute 42 seconds for 9 items and 17 minutes 44 seconds for 10 items.

Looking at these results in a different way, suppose a computer is capable of performing one million steps (units of work) in a second. (If the steps are small, such speeds might not be unreasonable with modern computers.) Then Figure 4-1 shows how long various algorithms would take, depending upon how much data were present and how many units of work were required to process the data.

More generally, from this table, it is clear that algorithms requiring n or n^2 or n^3 or perhaps n^4 operations to process n data items may be feasible, depending upon the number of data items and the actual length of the operations themselves. Algorithms requiring 2^n or 3^n or $n!$ or n^n operations are impractical even with a few pieces of data.

Each of these latter cases has the same characteristic seen earlier in the fable, where successive numbers increased by a factor of two or three or more for each successive value of n. In the fable, such payments forced the king from the throne. In computer processing, such levels of work are well beyond any imaginable computing system. Further, it should be noted that increasing the speed of computers by a factor of 10 or 100 or even 1,000 will have little impact on this problem. For example, from Figure 4-1, a thousand-fold increase in computer speed would reduce the processing time of 100 items for an $n!$ algorithm from 3.0×10^{146} years to a mere 3.0×10^{143} years. Either time will require an extended lunch break before results are available. (One could safely stay away for dinner and take in a show as well.)

In computing and mathematics, the term **combinatorial explosion** is used to describe this situation when work or required space increases by a factor of two or three or more for each successive value of n. From Figure 4-

Value	Number of Operations Required							
of N	n	n^2	n^3	n^4	2^n	3^n	$n!$	n^n
1	0.000001 seconds	0.000001 seconds	0.000001 seconds	0.000001 seconds	0.000002 seconds	0.000003 seconds	0.000001 seconds	0.000001 seconds
5	0.000005 seconds	0.000025 seconds	0.000125 seconds	0.000625 seconds	0.000032 seconds	0.000243 seconds	0.00012 seconds	0.003125 seconds
10	0.00001 seconds	0.0001 seconds	0.001 seconds	0.01 seconds	0.001024 seconds	0.059049 seconds	3.6288 seconds	2.778 hours
20	0.00002 seconds	0.0004 seconds	0.008 seconds	0.16 seconds	1.04858 seconds	58.1131 seconds	7.8218×10^4 years	3.37×10^{12} years
50	0.00005 seconds	0.0025 seconds	0.00125 seconds	0.625 seconds	26.1979 years	2.3×10^{10} years	9.77×10^{60} years	2.87×10^{70} years
75	0.000075 seconds	0.005625 seconds	0.421875 seconds	31.6406 seconds	1.2146×10^9 years	1.95×10^{22} years	1.95×10^{97} years	1.35×10^{127} years
200	0.0001 seconds	0.01 seconds	1.0000 second	1.667 minutes	4.0×10^{17} years	1.63×10^{34} years	3.0×10^{146} years	3.2×10^{186} years

NOTES:

1. This table assumes that the computer is capable of performing one million steps of the algorithm per second.

2. To gain additional insight on the length of some of these times, it is worthwhile to realize that scientists estimate the age of the universe to be between 10 and 20 billion years (between 1×10^{10} and 2×10^{10} years).

Figure 4-1:   Time Required to Complete Various Algorithms on Different Size Data Sets

1, it is clear that this combinatorial explosion must be avoided in designing feasible solutions for problems. Similarly, when the space requirements (for data or for corn payments) for an algorithm are exponential, then any machine will run out of space for all but the smallest data sets. Similarly, when the time required to perform an algorithm involves such expressions as exponentials (2^n, 3^n) or factorials ($n!$) or worse, then the solution will be impractical for any data sets containing over 10 or 20 or 30 items.

═══ CLASS P PROBLEMS ═══

While the Exhaustive Listing and Search approach potentially required $n!$ units of time to produce an ordered data set, the Selection Sort was much more efficient. (Actually, some other algorithms are significantly better still.) In this case, one solution of the problem took a prohibitively long time, but another approach seems reasonably manageable. This example raises the more general question, "If a problem has some solution, is it always possible to find a solution that is feasible?" That is, Chapter 3 already concluded that not all problems have solutions. However, ignoring these unsolvable problems, one might still hope that all solvable problems had solutions that were actually feasible.

Of course, any conclusions about this issue must depend upon the criteria one uses to determine the feasibility of a solution. Given the evidence in Figure 4-1, however, it would seem overly optimistic to consider a solution to be feasible if it required 2^n or 3^n or $n!$ or n^n units of work to process n data items. On the other hand, solutions requiring n or n^2 or n^3 units of work to process n items might reasonably be called feasible.

With this in mind, it is common to define a problem to be in **Class P** if the problem has some solution, where the number of steps to process n data items is (no more than) some polynomial involving n. For example, the problem of ordering a data set is in Class P since some solution (e.g., the Selection Sort) requires $(n^2+n)/2$ units of work, and $(n^2+n)/2$ or $\frac{1}{2}n^2+\frac{1}{2}n$ is a polynomial.

With this definition, one can be reasonably optimistic and decree that a problem has a feasible solution if it is Class P. Sorting data is feasible by this definition, for example. Similarly, many common computing applications, including the storage and retrieval of data, fall within the scope of this notion of feasibility. All of these common examples support the idea that problems within Class P may be considered to have practical solutions.[4] Conversely, considering Figure 4-1, it seems reasonably safe to conclude that problems outside Class P could not be solved in any acceptable amount of time. That is, if all solutions to a problem can be found where the work for n data items require more steps than can be described by any polynomial, then the work for all solutions must be exponentials (e.g., 2^n) or factorials (e.g., $n!$) or worse.

PROBLEMS REQUIRING EXPONENTIAL TIME

Now that Class P has been defined, it is reasonable to return to the question asked earlier, namely, "If a problem has some solution, is it always possible to find a solution that is feasible?" Following the discussion of Class P, one way to approach this question is to rephrase it by asking, "Are there any solvable problems that are not in Class P?" For example, one might ask, "Are there any problems whose solutions all require an exponential (e.g., 2^n) amount of work (or worse)?"

Unfortunately, the answers to these questions are "yes," just as the answer about the existence of unsolvable problems was affirmative. Some problems can only be solved in exponential time. One such problem, called the **Regular Expression Non-Universality Problem**, asks about specifications for strings of characters, although the details are somewhat too complex to describe here.[5] The analysis of this problem proves that not all problems can be solved in a reasonable amount of time, even when solutions to those problems are already known. Further, for these problems, expanding the capabilities of computers will yield only marginal returns, since increasing computer speed or capability by a factor of a few hundred or thousand still will not produce results for many thousands of years.

══ CHESS PROGRAMS ══

To understand why some approaches to problems typically become overwhelmed by the combinatorial explosion, it is instructive to consider how computers are programmed to play chess. While several types of solutions can be identified, the most common and successful all use the same basic approach:

- At each point in the game, the computer generates all possible moves, determines which approach is best, and selects this best looking move.
- To determine which of these moves is best, the computer looks at all responses that could be made to each move, assuming the opponent makes the best possible response.

As a practical matter, it can be difficult to determine which moves are best without looking at all possible future moves for both sides. In the jargon of game-playing programs, a **ply** is the term used to describe a move made by either player. Thus, two plies occur if you move and then your opponent makes a move. With three plies, you move, then your opponent moves, and then you move again. With this terminology, the basic idea of most chess programs is to look ahead in the game through as many plies as possible to determine the possible consequences of each move. Once these consequences are known, the best current move can be selected.

Unfortunately, however, the game of chess is complex, and it has been estimated that on the average a player will have to choose among about 20 possible moves. This number gives rise to the following rough analysis.

- In one ply, you will have about 20 possible moves.
- For a second ply, an opponent will have about 20 possible responses for each move you might make. Thus, there are about 20×20 or 400 possibilities at the end of two plies.
- For each of these 400 possibilities, you will have a choice of roughly 20 responses. This gives $20 \times 20 \times 20$ or 20^3 = 8,000 possibilities at the end of three plies.

$\vdots$

- At the end of i plies, there are roughly 20^i possible move sequences.

Thus, the number of possible move sequences is an exponential function of the number of plies considered. Since this number increases very quickly, chess-playing programs can never hope to consider all possible consequences of every particular move; if a typical game involves about 50 moves, this analysis suggests that a computer would have to consider roughly 20^{50} different move sequences before it could choose the best response to the first move by an opponent. To put this in some perspective, scientists estimate that the age of the universe is between 10 and 20 billion years. Assuming 20 billion years, a computer would have had to analyze about 1.3×10^{47} chess moves per second to respond by now to an initial move made at the birth of the universe. In contrast, the fastest modern computers can perform only about 10^7 to 10^8 instructions per second, and there is no prospect that increases in computer speed will have much real impact on this problem.

Since such numbers are so large, modern chess playing programs must restrict what moves are considered. A particularly common approach is to look ahead only a specified number of plies. For example, several of the best programs currently available may look ahead 8 or 9 plies. Other programs may only consider some possible moves instead of all of them. Libraries of common board positions may also allow the machine to restrict the number of moves it must consider.

Regardless of how the range of chess moves are restricted, this approach to playing chess is a particularly good example of limitations that arise due to the combinatorial explosion. Each additional ply increases the number of moves to be considered by a factor of about 20. The consequences are parallel to what the king encountered in the fable. Clever people find ways to increase the capabilities for one more ply (or one more square of corn payments), but there can be little hope that a general solution can be found using this approach. Any completely successful approach will have to proceed differently (e.g., the king may abdicate).

═══ NP PROBLEMS ═══

Up to this point, it has been possible to identify three categories of problems, as illustrated in Figure 4-2. Some problems, such as the Halting Problem, are known to be unsolvable; some problems, such as the Regular Expression Non-Universality Problem, are known to require an exponential number of steps, so solutions are normally not feasible; some problems, such as the Sorting Problem, have solutions where the number of steps can be expressed as a polynomial, and so are feasible to solve. With these conclusions, one might ask if there were any problems that were *between* Class P and the exponential class in some sense. Are there some problems that do not seem to have feasible solutions in a traditional sense but which are not known to be infeasible either? For example, one might wonder if some problems could be solved in a reasonable amount of time if enough computers were allowed to work together on the same problem.

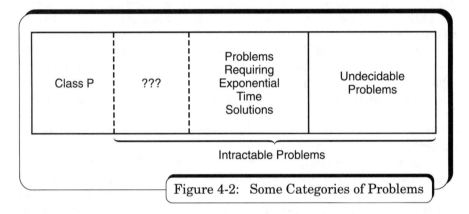

Figure 4-2:   Some Categories of Problems

As a simple example, consider the Exhaustive Listing and Search solution to the Sorting Problem, mentioned earlier. In this approach, all possible permutations of the data were considered, and an ordered one was selected. If this approach were tried with many different computers, then it might be possible for each computer to try a different permutation and check if it was ordered. Once some computer found a sorted permutation, this computer might report its finding to a central machine, where the result could be displayed. In this approach, information must flow between a central, controlling machine and the many other computers, and the work might proceed in three basic steps.

1. The original data are sent to all available computers.

2. Each computer picks a distinct permutation of the data and checks if that permutation is ordered.

3. If a computer determines that its permutation is ordered, then it sends a message back to the central machine indicating that this specific permutation of data works.

In reviewing the time required for this approach, it is worthwhile to note that the overall amount of work here exceeds what may be needed with only one machine, since steps 1 and 3 require data communication that is unnecessary when only one computer is working. On the other hand, if enough computers are available, it may be possible to spread this work over many computers with a resulting overall gain in time.[6]

To be more precise in this analysis, steps 1 and 3 each require that n pieces of data are transmitted from one machine to one or more others. Typically one piece of data is sent at a time, so overall this requires n units of time for each step. (In step 1, as with a radio or television broadcast, the central machine may send the data to many other machines at once, and no time is lost by having many computers obtain the same data from the central machine.)

Continuing the analysis, each machine must consider a distinct permutation of data and then check if the data in that permutation are ordered. Normally, the consideration of a single permutation of data can be done very quickly, so this step too can be done in few units of time, perhaps $2n$.

Putting these remarks together, it would seem that this approach to sorting could be done in roughly $n + 2n + n = 4n$ units of time if enough computers were available to help. Thus, while this Exhaustive Listing and Search approach to sorting requires too many steps with only one computer, this approach might work effectively if enough machines were available.

This motivates the definition that a problem is in **Class NP** if it has some solution that requires no more than a polynomial number of steps, given enough computers. As an example, the previous discussion shows that the Sorting Problem is in Class NP. Alternatively, this same conclusion could be reached more easily by noting that the Selection Sort uses one processor and requires no more than a polynomial number of steps. Since the problem can be done efficiently with one processor, it certainly can be done efficiently with many processors (just let one computer do all the work and let any other computers remain idle). Following this same argument, any problem in Class P will also be in Class NP. Any problem that it is feasible to solve with one computer is certainly feasible to solve with many.

THE TRAVELING SALESPERSON PROBLEM

Another problem in Class NP is commonly known as the **Traveling Salesperson Problem**.[7] In this problem, a salesperson is responsible for visiting a number of cities. In order to complete this task efficiently, the salesperson wants to find a route of minimal cost that goes through each city exactly once before returning to the starting point.

As an example, the map in Figure 4-3 shows several cities in the midwest, together with the cost involved for flying from one city to another. Thus, the figure shows that it costs $226 to fly from Des Moines to Chicago. On

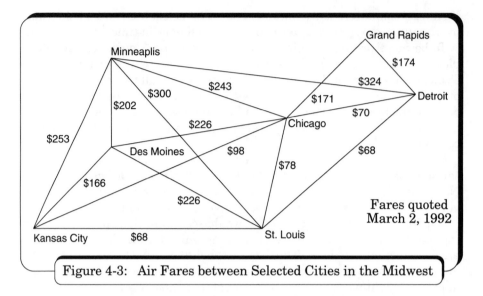

Figure 4-3:   Air Fares between Selected Cities in the Midwest

the other hand, there are no direct flights between Des Moines and Grand Rapids.

Now suppose that a salesperson starts from Des Moines. As a first question, one might ask whether the person can go to each of these cities exactly once and then return back to Des Moines. In reviewing the figure, this can be done in several ways. For example, two routes are:

1. Des Moines ⇒ Chicago ⇒ Grand Rapids ⇒ Detroit
   ⇒ St. Louis ⇒ Kansas City ⇒ Minneapolis ⇒ Des Moines

2. Des Moines ⇒ Minneapolis ⇒ Detroit ⇒ Grand Rapids
   ⇒ Chicago ⇒ St. Louis ⇒ Kansas City ⇒ Des Moines

Then, once one knows that a specific route is possible, it is reasonable to ask which route incurs the least cost.

One solution to this problem can follow the same basic approach used in the Exhaustive Listing and Search Solution for sorting. In particular, each possible route (or permutation of cities) might be considered. In some cases, there may not be direct flights between some cities, so some routes might not be possible (one cannot go directly from Minneapolis to Grand Rapids, for example, so any potential route requiring this trip must be ruled out).

For each route, a cost can then be computed and these costs can be compared. If many computers are available, initial data could be sent to each computer (in step 1), routes and costs could be computed (in step 2), and results from different routes could be compared (in step 3). While this data communication (in steps 1 and 3) is significantly harder here than in the sorting discussion earlier, it turns out that it still can be done in a reasonable (polynomial-steps) amount of time. This solution to the Traveling Salesperson Problem, therefore, is feasible if enough computers are available, and one may conclude that the Traveling Salesperson Problem is in Class NP.

Unlike the Sorting Problem, however, there are no known solutions to the Traveling Salesperson Problem that are fundamentally more efficient. Some improvements can be made to the basic approach of trying all possible routes through the various cities, but no solutions are known that require only one computer and only a polynomial number of steps. Thus, while the Traveling Salesperson Problem is in Class NP, no evidence suggests that it is in Class P. No known, feasible solutions to this problem require only one computer. On the other hand, no one has proven that feasible solutions to the Traveling Salesperson Problem do not exist.

This discussion leads to Figure 4-4, which refines Figure 4-2. Problems can be classified as being unsolvable, as requiring exponential time, as requiring polynomial time if enough processors are available (Class NP), and as requiring polynomial time with only one processor (Class P). Further, Class NP contains Class P, and the Traveling Salesperson Problem is in Class NP with no evidence that it also is in Class P. However, no one knows for sure that Class NP actually contains problems that are not in Class P. In fact, a major unanswered question in computer science is whether $P = NP$.

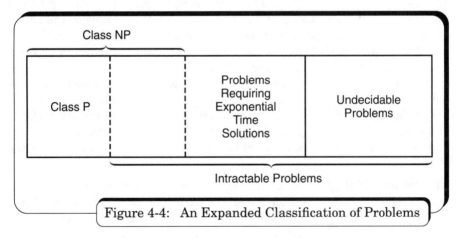

Figure 4-4:   An Expanded Classification of Problems

═══ NP-COMPLETE PROBLEMS ═══

While both Class P and Class NP may be considered to contain problems with feasible solutions, any problems in Class NP that are outside Class

P may require very large numbers of resources. For example, in the solution of the Traveling Salesperson Problem described earlier, a separate computer was needed for each possible route the salesperson might make through the n cities, and this might require $n!$ computers. For $n = 10$, therefore, this algorithm would require $1,612,800$ processors, and for $n = 12$, this number would be in the billions. While some efficiencies might reduce this number somewhat, it would seem prudent to consider any such solutions somewhat impractical. Real constraints on the number of computers available, therefore, provide a major motivation to learn if more feasible solutions do exist for problems in Class NP.

To investigate whether problems in Class NP also lie in Class P, an interesting approach proceeds in two basic steps:

1. Translate all problems in Class NP efficiently into a specified problem.
2. Investigate the solutions to this special problem.

If this special problem can be solved efficiently, then any problem in class NP also has an efficient solution. (First, efficiently translate any given problem to the special one, and then efficiently solve the special one.)

In the jargon of computer science, a problem S is said to be **NP-Hard** if any problem in Class NP can be translated efficiently into S. (More precisely, a translation must be made in a way that requires no more than a polynomial number of steps.) If S is also within Class NP itself, then S is said to be **NP-Complete**. With this terminology, any efficient solution to an NP-Complete problem would yield an efficient solution to every problem in Class NP, and one would know that Classes NP and P were the same. On the other hand, if one could show that some NP-Complete problem did not possess an efficient (polynomial-time) solution, then it would be clear that Class NP was strictly bigger than Class P.

On the surface, it might seem hopeless to show that every possible problem in Class NP may be reduced to a specific one. After all, it is hard even to imagine all possible problems, much less to prove something about them. However, in 1971, Stephen Cook did precisely this by showing that all problems in Class NP could be reduced to a problem, called the **Satisfiability Problem**.

The Satisfiability Problem. While a formal statement of the Satisfiability Problem is somewhat technical, the basic idea is reasonably intuitive. In the field of logic, it is common to study logical statements, such as

$$(A\ And\ (Not\ B))\ Implies\ (C\ Or\ (D\ And\ E)).$$

In such expressions, A, B, C, D, and E are considered to be variables (or statements) that are *True* or *False*, and these statements are connected in various ways using such words as *And*, *Or*, *Not*, *Implies*, and *Equals*. For example, suppose

- *A* represents the statement "the temperature is above 80 degrees,"

- *B* represents the statement "it is raining,"

- *C* represents the statement "I will go swimming,"

- *D* represents the statement "I will stay inside an air-conditioned building," and

- *E* represents the statement "I will read a book."

Then the expression (*A And* (*NotB*)) *Implies* (*C Or* (*D And E*)) could be interpreted as saying, "If the temperature is above 80 degrees and it is not raining, then either I will go swimming or I will stay inside where it is air-conditioned and read a book."

In considering any such expression, the overall statement may be either true or false. For example, if I go swimming, then the expression is true, but if I go outside to water the garden, then the expression may be false. With this background, the Satisfiability Problem asks whether, given a logical expression, values can be given to the variables (e.g., *A*, *B*, *C*, *D*, and *E*) so that the overall expression is true.

To solve this problem, one approach considers all possible values for the variables and then determines if the overall expression has the desired true value. (This is not unlike the Exhaustive Listing and Search approach for sorting and the list-all-routes solution to the Traveling Salesperson Problem.) Since each collection of possible values could be tried on a separate computer with any true values reported, this solution can be done quite efficiently if enough computers are available, and the Satisfiability Problem is in Class NP.

The significance of Cook's work[8] involved showing that all other problems in Class NP could be translated to this Satisfiability Problem in an efficient way. Thus, not only was this problem in Class NP, but this problem also could be used to solve all other such problems. This proves that the Satisfiability Problem is NP-Complete.

In the years since 1971, the Traveling Salesperson Problem and many other problems in Class NP also have been shown to be NP-Complete (often by showing how to translate the Satisfiability Problem into these other problems), and today a rather large number of problems are known to be NP-Complete.

Is P = NP? For any of these NP-Complete problems, it is still unknown if efficient solutions can be found using one processor. Each of these problems is related, however, in that an efficient solution to any one of them would result in feasible solutions to them all. While the discovery of such an efficient solution would have major consequences, most computer scientists seem to believe that such solutions do not exist, and $P \neq NP$. (After all, if efficient solutions really exist, it is not unreasonable to expect that some of them would have been found by now.) However, it remains to be seen if this view is correct; perhaps a reader of this book will find a new, efficient approach to the Traveling Salesperson Problem and show therefore that P and NP include exactly the same problems.

═══ SUMMARY ═══

1. Class P contains those problems that have solutions that can be run on a single computer in no more than an polynomial number of units of time. That is, if $p(n)$ is the amount of time required to solve a problem involving n data items, then $p(n)$ is bounded by some polynomial. As an example, the Sorting Problem is in Class P.

2. Class NP contains those problems that can be solved in a polynomial number of time units, assuming enough computers are available.

3. Class NP contains Class P, but it is unknown if there are any problems in Class NP that are outside Class P. For example, both the Traveling Salesperson Problem and the Satisfiability Problem are known to be in Class NP, but no polynomial-time solutions requiring only one computer are known for either of them.

4. Problems outside Class NP may be regarded as being unfeasible.

   • Some unfeasible problems are solvable, but all solutions require exponential time or worse. For example, all solutions to the Regular Expression Non-Universality Problem require exponential time at least.

   • Some problems, such as the Halting Problem, have no solutions at all.

5. NP-Hard problems have the special property that all other problems in Class NP can be translated efficiently to them. When such problems also are in Class NP, they are called NP-Complete. For example, it has been shown that any problem in Class NP can be translated efficiently (in no more than a polynomial number of steps) into either appropriate expressions for the Satisfiability Problem or into questions about traveling salespeople. Thus, both the Satisfiability Problem and the Traveling Salesperson Problem are NP-Complete.

6. If an efficient (polynomial-time) solution were found to any NP-Hard or NP-Complete problem, then efficient solutions also would be available for any problem in Class NP. Unfortunately, to date, no such efficient solutions have been found. On the other hand, no one has proven that

such solutions do not exist, so there is still hope that such solutions eventually will be found.

$\equiv$ CONCLUSIONS AND IMPLICATIONS $\equiv$

This chapter argued that problems in Class P can actually be solved in a reasonable amount of time, and problems in Class NP similarly may be feasible if enough processors are available. It is unknown whether Classes P and NP include exactly the same problems, and one can speculate about whether all problems in Class NP can be solved in a feasible amount of time. Problems outside of these classes, however, almost certainly cannot be solved in an acceptable amount of time, except perhaps in some special cases.

While this analysis of problems has technical significance for computing, the broader implications are even more important. Chapter 3 already noted that some problems simply cannot be solved. Even when problems are solvable, however, this chapter shows that some solutions will take too long. Expanding the speed and capabilities of computers may help in some cases, but for many problems the combinatorial explosion renders many solutions worthless in any practical sense.

When the number of steps required to complete solutions involves formulae such as 2^n or $n!$, the work required to process data becomes unbelievably large, and improvements in technology will have only a marginal effect. For example:

- for algorithms requiring 2^n operations to process n items, a 10-fold increase in processing speed will allow n to increase by about 3, and

- for algorithms requiring 3^n or $n!$ or more operations, a 10-fold increase in processing speed will have even less effect.

In such situations, one cannot expect an increase in technology to provide solutions to problems. Even when problems are solvable in theory, the combinatorial explosion can effectively prevent solutions from being completed in one's lifetime (or perhaps even in the next few thousand years). The combinatorial explosion provides a significant limit on the capabilities of computing.

═══ DISCUSSION QUESTIONS ═══

4.1 This chapter contains a mix of major concepts and technical details. For each section within the chapter, identify the main concept(s), and then write a high-level review or outline of the chapter, omitting the technical details.

4.2 The first part of this chapter presents several different formulae for payments, based upon the size of a chess board. Determine how many kernels of corn would be required for borads with 20 or 50 or 100 squares for each of payment algorithms given.

4.3 The Selection Sort

  a. Write out 20 numbers in random order. Then follow the outline of the Selection Sort to arrange them in ascending order.

  b. Count the number of steps required to apply the Selection Sort to a collection of 5, 10, and 15 randomly ordered numbers.

4.4 Exhaustive Listing and Search

  a. Write out four distinct numbers in random order. Then write out all 24 permutations of these numbers. Describe how you found all of these permutations.

  b. How many permutations would there be for collections of 3, 5, 6, 7, or 8 distinct numbers? (Do not try to list all such permutations!)

  c. Describe an algorithm that could generate all permutations of a collection of distinct numbers. As an example, apply your algorithm to a collection of three distinct numbers and to the four numbers you used in part (a).

4.5 Ordering a Deck of Cards

  a. Shuffle a deck of cards. Then put the cards back into order (note you will need to decide what it means for a card deck to be ordered.)

  b. Formalize your approach in part (a) to describe an algorithm for sorting a deck of cards.

  c. Suppose you applied your algorithm in part (b) to a collection of n cards (perhaps part of a deck). Determine how many times you handle (or consult) each card. From this analysis, determine if the number of steps required by your algorithm is a polynomial.

4.6 Consider ordering a deck of cards by a Selection Sort or by exhaustive listing and search. How many steps would be required to finish each of these sorting algorithms on a randomly ordered deck of cards. If each step could be completed in one second, how long would each of these algorithms take?

4.7 Figure 4-3 gives the costs charged for flying between several midwestern cities.

   a. Find the least expensive routing that allows someone to go to all of these cities exactly once before returning home.

   b. Suppose some additional air links were added to Figure 4-3, so that direct flights were possible between any two cities listed. (Make up some fares that seem reasonable for these new flights.) Now find the least expensive routing covering each city once, and prove that your answer is the cheapest.

   c. Compare your approaches to finding the solution in parts (a) and (b). Did you use some special properties of the graph in part (a) that you could not use in part (b)?

   d. Discuss how your solution to part (b) might be simplified if you could organize a team of people to help find the least expensive route.

4.8 This chapter's discussion of the combinatorial explosion describes five different formulae that might have been used by the king in paying Paul. In these formulae, the number of kernels of corn paid for the ith square of a chess board were 2^i, $2i - 1$, i^2, $i!$ (i factorial), and i^i. Compute each of these values for a variety of values of i and then plot the results with i on one axis and the number of kernels on the other axis. (Be sure all results are plotted on the same axes.) Describe in words how the graphs for the various formulae compare.

4.9 NP-Completeness

   a. Define what is meant by saying "a problem is NP-Hard" and "a problem is NP-Complete."

   b. Could a problem be NP-Hard without also being NP-Complete? Conversely, could a problem be NP-Complete without also being NP-Hard?

   c. Why do you think a distinction is made between these two concepts?

NOTES

1   The USDA and the University of Illinois have developed a measure, called
     the *Corn Yield Calculator*, to determine quantities of corn. According to this
     measure, a bushel averages 72,800 kernels of corn.

2   To put this number in perspective, the world's annual production for corn in
     the mid-1980s was roughly 17.7 billion bushels a year. Thus, even in modern
     times, it would take roughly 6,215 years for the world to grow enough corn for
     payment for this last square. Paul's entire payment would take about twice
     this long, or about 12,430 years, using modern technology.

3   The following sections combine some technical detail with a discussion of more
     general concepts and issues. On first reading, you should not become bogged
     down with the details to the point that the main arguments are missed.

4   Some people might argue that even this notion of feasibility is overly generous,
     since polynomials, such as $n^{25} + 50000n$, may yield very large values for even
     modest values of n. An algorithm requiring this much work to process n items
     would require over 32 million steps to process just 2 items, for example. Even
     with such results being possible, however, the current discussion will adopt
     the optimistic perspective that any problems in Class P can be solved in a
     reasonable amount of time.

5   A reasonably concise description of the problem may be found in Henry M.
     Walker, *Computer Science 2: Principles of Software Engineering, Data Types,
     and Algorithms*, Scott, Foresman and Company, Glenview, Illinois, 1989, pp.
     525–527. Details that prove that solutions to the problem require at least
     exponential time may be found in A. R. Meyer and L. J. Stockmeyer, "The
     Equivalence Problem for Regular Expressions with Squaring Requires Expo-
     nential Time," *Proceedings of the 13th Annual Symposium on Switching and
     Automata Theory*, Long Beach, California, IEEE Computer Society, 1972, pp.
     125–129.

6   One might consider this approach a computerized version of the old adage,
     "Many hands make light work."

7   Historically, this problem was called the Traveling Salesman Problem. While
     references in the literature frequently use this name, the more inclusive term
     is used in this text.

8   For more details, see S. A. Cook, "The Complexity of Theorem-Proving Pro-
     cedures," *Proceedings of the Third Annual ACM Symposium on the Theory of
     Computing*, New York: Association for Computing Machinery, 1971, pp. 151–
     158.

PART III
Hardware

Next Week's Lesson at the Silicon Valley Assembly of God: How in the Beginning Moses Brought Down 25 Commandments, but 15 Were In Cross Linked Sectors

From a Sunday news magazine report in the *The Dallas Morning News*, November 10, 1991:

"Lutheran pastor John C. Hildner recently told an Arlington seminar what religious message might be appropriate in our modern, user-friendly world. 'He might ask, "Why do you see the byte that is in your brother's eye, but don't see the megabyte that is in your own eye?" ' the Rev. Hildner said. 'And the message probably would refer to sin of transgression as an "imparity error" or suggest at confession, "Fail, retry or abort." ' Unable to resist a pun, Mr. Hildner added an Old Testament allusion to computer lingo: 'Don't forget, in the story of Abraham's willing sacrifice of his son, Isaac, God supplied him with enough ram.' "

—From Bill Howard, "Abort, Retry, Fail?" *PC Magazine*, Vol. 11, No. 6, March 31, 1992, p. 454.

When computer systems perform a task, it is often useful to separate the activity into two interrelated, but logically distinct realms: hardware and software. Hardware consists of the mechanical and electrical machinery that physically does the work. A keyboard sends electrical signals when fingers press keys; sensors may determine levels of heat or radioactivity or fluid velocity; printers may push typing elements against a carbon ribbon to stamp letters on paper. Hardware acts in tangible or measurable ways. Software, on the other hand, contains the instructions that tell the hardware what to do when. Software provides the controls and directions that the hardware carries out.

Both hardware and software, of course, must function properly in harmony for an overall computer system to execute its assigned tasks correctly. In a smoothly functioning system, software provides logically reasoned guidance, and the hardware responds by performing appropriate specific activities. Malfunctions or flaws in either may lead to errors in the work of the overall system.

While hardware and software are interrelated in a variety of ways, many of their characteristics are quite different. In many ways, the development process for hardware is better understood than for software, and reliability checks may be incorporated into hardware more easily. It may even be argued that some types of hardware are fundamentally simpler than the corresponding software. As a result, the development process for hardware is more highly refined than for software, and various inventive techniques are available to help resolve many obstacles and limitations. Some constraints, however, can be shown to be more fundamental.

Part III, with Chapter 5, explores some of these characteristics and issues related to hardware. Software issues are considered in Part IV.

Tracy Kidder tells the story of how the last major hardware bug was found in a new Data General machine. As the deadline for bringing the machine to market approached, the designers were frustrated by their long-standing inability to find a "flakey" bug in the ALU (Arithmetic Logic Unit) of Gallifrey, their prototype machine. A flakey bug is one that the debuggers can't figure out how to reproduce. In this case, the designers had spent days trying to catch the bug when it occurred, but had been stymied by its unpredictability, its apparently randomness.

On October 6 the vice president, Carl Carman, came down to the lab as usual, and they told him about the flakey.

The ALU was sitting outside Gallifrey's frame, on the extender. Gallifrey was running a low-level program. Carman said, "Hmmm." He walked over to the computer and, to the engineers' horror, he grasped the ALU board by its edges and shook it. At that instant, Gallifrey failed.

They knew where the problem lay now. Guyer and Holberger and Rasala spent most the next day replacing all the sockets that held the chips in the center of the ALU, and when they finished, the flakey was gone for good.

"Carman did it," said Holberger. "He got it to fail by beating it up."

—From Nathaniel Borenstein, *Programming As If People Mattered*, Princeton University Press, 1991, p. 37. This passage, in turn, quotes, Tracy Kidder, *The Soul of a New Machine*, Little, Brown and Company, 1981.

Hardware and Reliability

A computer's hardware involves the mechanical and electrical machinery that physically performs operations, as instructed by a user or programmer. Some common mechanical components may include keyboards (which allow people to type data), printers, and storage devices (such as disk drives or compact disk readers). In industrial or experimental environments, such components may include sensors (to determine levels of heat, radiation, electrical voltage, or fluid flow) and controls to operate motors, regulate machinery, or administer medicines to patients. While this list of mechanical devices is far from complete, it does suggest something about the wide range of mechanical parts that may be part of a computerized system. In most cases, these devices contain parts that move together to perform a specified operation.

Electrical components include an equally wide range of devices and types. The heart of many of these components involves a collection of chips, which are intricate collections of circuits that are manufactured as a single unit. Chips normally are connected together in groups. For example, several chips may be mounted together on circuit boards, and these boards then may be combined by plugging them into specially designed cabinets. Since chips, boards, and cabinets contain electrical components, they often do not contain moving parts, although they may be affected by mechanical components through such factors as heat or vibration.

At a somewhat more general and elementary level, some characteristics of the mechanical and the electrical components that make up a computer's hardware may be reviewed by considering three basic questions:

1. What is involved in the initial design and construction of the hardware?

2. How fast can hardware perform its assigned tasks?

3. Once hardware is built, what issues of maintenance can be identified?

The following pages investigate each of these questions in turn.

HARDWARE DESIGN AND CONSTRUCTION

The design and construction of hardware, of course, can be very complex and require much technical expertise and insight. For much computing equipment, however, all work depends upon a very few basic circuits, which manipulate voltages. Normally, computers are designed so that circuits are in one of two basic states: a location has a relatively high voltage (typically 3 to 5 volts) or a circuit carries a relatively low voltage (close to 0 volts). Frequently these states are notated with a 1 or a 0, respectively, so the notation "1" indicates that a circuit has a relatively high voltage, while "0" specifies that no voltage can be detected at a particular location at a given moment.

With this notation, most computer chips depend upon only three basic circuits, called **gates**. In each case, one or more circuits lead into the circuit or gate, and one output circuit results. (Figure 5- 1 shows the logical structure of these gates.)

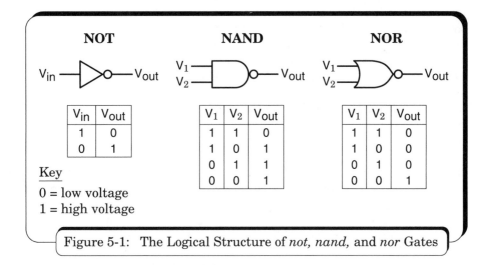

Figure 5-1:   The Logical Structure of *not, nand,* and *nor* Gates

- A *not* gate reverses the voltage state for a circuit. If the input circuit is high, then a *not* gate produces a low voltage output, and conversely. At a logical level, $V_{out} = 0$ when $V_{in} = 1$, and conversely $V_{out} = 1$ when $V_{in} = 0$.

- A *nand* gate has two input circuits V_1 and V_2 and produces a single output circuit V_{out}, which is a high voltage unless both input voltages are high. Logically, $V_{out} = 0$ when both $V_1 = 1$ and $V_2 = 1$, and $V_{out} = 1$ otherwise.

- A *nor* gate also has two input circuits V_1 and V_2 and produces a single output circuit V_{out}. Here, V_{out} is a high voltage only if both input voltages are low. Logically, $V_{out} = 1$ when both $V_1 = 0$ and $V_2 = 0$, and $V_{out} = 0$ otherwise.

While these circuits are quite simple, it turns out that they provide sufficient flexibility and capability to create virtually all other logical circuits required within a computer. Further, these three gates can be made very cheaply and combined easily in great numbers to create chips. Thus, most complex chips and computers can be considered as being built from these three simple starting points.

As an elementary analogy, consider the structures children make from blocks (such as Lego's). Packages contain many blocks, based on a very few basic shapes. Several packages supply an almost limitless supply of blocks, and the fun and challenge is to fit the basic shapes together in inventive ways to build complex buildings, bridges, roads, or even cities. Eventually, large, intricate structures emerge from a very few basic shapes.

Pursuing this analogy a bit further, in first starting to build, a child often has a general image of what he or she wants to construct. Although rarely written formally, this general image may serve the purpose of rough specifications. As the work progresses, it may become clear that the initial specifications cannot be filled (e.g., a bridge span may be too long to hold together without additional supports). Modifications and adjustments in goals or specifications may be needed – in some cases, a project may be beyond what is either possible or feasible to build. Even with these cautions, however, it is remarkable how extensive a masterpiece you can build using many blocks based on a very few basic shapes.

While it would be unfair to conclude from this analogy that building computers from basic circuits is child's play, it is correct to view a complex computer chip as being built from hundreds or thousands of simple circuits following well-established construction principles. As with building blocks, one cannot expect to meet all possible specifications for chips by putting circuits together, but a very wide range of capabilities are possible.

Some Major Advances for Designing Chips. Over the years, the process of designing and building these complex chips has been refined, and now several aids are available to help in the process. In fact, hardware engineering now has advanced to the point that, given the specifications, chips can be designed and manufactured so that the first attempts are often correct. That is, the process of developing chips has progressed to the point that few mistakes find their way even into initial prototypes.[1] While many factors have contributed to this high success rate, two areas of particular note involve computer-assisted design (CAD) and formal verification techniques.

Computer-assisted design (CAD) uses a computer to store, manipulate, and display information during the design (and sometimes the manufacture) of chips and other hardware. For example, a computer may store specifications and then compare them with the capabilities currently available in a chip under development. The CAD system may detect discrepancies with the specifications, and it may display a graphical schematic of the chip under development. In adding circuits to the chip, the CAD system may allow the designer to draw connections or components and insert previously developed and tested chip parts into sections of a new chip. Thus, CAD systems provide ways to automate the development process of performing routine tasks, retrieving and inserting past designs, testing results, and setting up equipment that will actually manufacture chips. Such systems not only speed up the design process, but they also help designers check that chips under development will meet their specifications. The result is a greatly increased capacity to develop chips quickly and correctly.

A second significant area that has helped in the development of correct chips uses formal, mathematical reasoning to prove logically that a given chip design actually meets its specifications. Here, the approach is much the same as you might have encountered in a formal geometry class, where results or theorems are proven based upon specified axioms. For example, in geometry, one might prove that the diagonals of a rhombus are perpendicular by considering various triangles formed by the sides and the diagonals. In a proof, various sides are found to be congruent to each other, and then triangles are shown to be congruent by a formal argument. Finally, a logical argument allows one to conclude that the measures of certain angles are 90 degrees. Throughout the proof, detailed arguments lead to certain conclusions, and these conclusions are combined to yield the final result or theorem.

Of course, proofs involving chips and their specifications naturally depend upon somewhat different axioms and arguments than might be found in geometry. The basic approach, however, is quite similar, and in recent years, remarkable results have been obtained in proving the correctness of some chip designs. The next chapter describes some particular successes in further detail.

To summarize, these and other advances in the design process now allow much hardware to be developed and manufactured with a high degree of confidence that it meets given specifications. While hardware clearly cannot be made to do everything, modern engineering techniques do provide highly efficient and effective ways to design and produce hardware that meets a wide range of specifications. The development of hardware, therefore, often is not the limiting factor in determining the capabilities of computer systems.

Maintenance Issues. Unfortunately, once equipment is constructed and functioning smoothly, there is no guarantee that it will continue to work over time. Hardware can wear out, and parts can fail. For example, friction can wear down moving parts, and environmental factors, such as vibration and heat, can cause further deterioration of equipment. Of course, when wear and tear can be anticipated, regular maintenance schedules can be developed to address these issues. (For example, you might change the oil in a car every 3,000 miles as a preventive measure to help keep an engine working properly. Similarly, some early settlers of wilderness areas are reported to have bathed regularly every six months, whether they needed it or not.) Other factors are less predictable, and part failure is always a possibility in any hardware.

In this regard, it is worthwhile to note that issues of wear and deterioration apply to hardware, but not to software. Equipment is subject to mechanical or electrical failure, and in the context of hardware, the term **maintenance** is used both for the detection, correction, and replacement of failed parts and for the periodic work done to prevent failures.

In contrast, software involves the instructions that control the functioning of equipment. Once these instructions are correctly determined according to given specifications, then the logic should not change for those specifications. Thus, the software world does not require preventive maintenance to anticipate wear and tear in logic. Instead, for software, the term maintenance reflects the need to change instructions to meet new or revised specifications or to correct errors.

The notion of maintenance, therefore, has a fundamentally different meaning in the context of hardware or software. Hardware maintenance will be discussed more extensively later in this chapter when considering reliability, while software maintenance is addressed in Chapter 6.

═══ SPEED ═══

The next issue that frequently arises in connection with hardware involves how fast a task can be performed. For example, consider the factors that limit how quickly a person can be moved from one point to another. Clearly a major variable involves the mode of transportation under consideration. If the person must rely upon his or her own muscles, then the question must focus upon how fast a person can walk or run without mechanical assistance. While details involve matters of conditioning, training, and distance, speeds fall into a reasonably narrow range (perhaps 4 to 15 miles per hour). In contrast, if a different approach is taken to the transportation problem, then the focus changes to how fast a car (or a train, bus, plane, or spacecraft) can be made to move. In the atmosphere, speed may be limited (at least in populated areas) by the speed of sound, to avoid problems with sonic booms. At the furthest extreme, one might even consider speeds seen in the movies or on the television program *Star Trek*, where people are transported using force fields, light, or electricity. While such travel seems fanciful at best, even here science indicates that movement is limited by the speed of light.

This travel example suggests several basic principles relating to the speed at which work can be done. First, speed may depend upon the type of technology used. For a given approach, it may be possible to refine how work is done, giving some improvements in speed. Track athletes learn how to improve their times by refining their technique. Second, it may be impossible to improve the performance of a given technology beyond a certain point. Other factors, such as the speed of sound or light, may provide absolute limits. When such limitations appear, work may allow improvements in a technology that bring it ever closer to the best possible. Machines may be refined, so that they perform the best they are capable of, but these improvements cannot overcome the fundamental obstacles. Third, dramatic improvements in speed often require different approachs to a problem. People move from point to point faster in cars than when walking (except perhaps during rush hour in major cities).

The Speed of Light. Within computers, of course, data move from place to place by electrical impulses, and these impulses cannot move faster than the speed of light, about 2.997×10^{10} centimeters per second.[2] Historically, these data transmission speeds have been sufficiently fast that they have had little bearing upon the speed of computers. Computer speeds have not been limited in any significant way by the speed of data transmission.

Expanding upon this point, computer speeds typically are measured in the number of machine instructions that can be performed in a second and speeds are often measured in MIPS, one million instructions executed per second. Figure 5-2 shows that, over the past several decades, there has been a reasonably consistent pattern of the speeds of various computers increasing by a factor of 10 every six to seven years. More specifically, the figure gives the number of additions that modern mechanical or electrical computers could perform in a second for a wide variety of machines. While the numbers are different, similar patterns are obtained for the number of multiplications per second.

Today, the fastest personal computers may reach speeds of 20 MIPS, and the fastest supercomputers perform several billion instructions per second. With a speed of one billion instructions per second, however, any single instruction takes about 6×10^{-10} seconds, and in this time a piece of data can move only about 18 centimeters (about seven inches) even if it moves at the speed of light. With such execution speeds, therefore, there is a limit as to how far data may be stored away from a processor without slowing the machine down. With another order of magnitude increase in processing speed, data could move no more than 1.8 centimeters (about three-fours of an inch) in the time required for an instruction to be performed. (The dotted

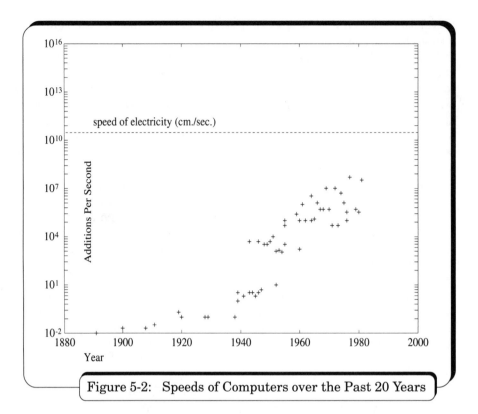

Figure 5-2:   Speeds of Computers over the Past 20 Years

horizontal line in Figure 5-2 also shows how many centimeters electricity can go in one second. If electricity must travel a centimeter to complete processing of one operation, then this line represents a maximum number of operations that could be performed in one second.) Such computations suggest that the speed of electricity may well become a factor in the development of future computers. It is no longer the case that increases in speed depend solely upon the inventiveness of people to design circuits. Now the speed of light can affect where data can be stored and how fast they can be stored and retrieved. With this limitation, it is unreasonable to expect the curve in Figure 5-2 to continue to show similar speed increases in coming years. Refinements certainly can be anticipated, but physical limitations must now be considered in ways that did not matter previously.

Parallelism. While machines themselves are limited by the speed of light, processing speeds sometimes can be improved if several processes can be done at once. There may be a limit on what one processor can do, but perhaps several processors could work at once. This is one of the primary motivations for **parallel processing** or **distributed computing**, where several distinct processors all work simultaneously on different parts of the same problem.

In parallel processing, a common approach involves dividing a task into several independent parts, and then assigning each part to a different processor. These separate parts can then be combined at the end of the job to yield an overall result. For example, such an approach can be very effective in the processing of weather data, since information for a region can be divided into separate geographical areas, and one processor may analyze the data for each region. With care, the work for one region and one time period will not affect computations for other regions at that same time, and separate computers may work together on different parts of the problem.

While this use of parallelism can be very effective in increasing computational speeds, this approach only works when the separate computations are independent. If computation B cannot proceed until computation A is complete, then there is little advantage in assigning separate processors to each task. One processor can work on A, but the processor working on B must remain idle until A is done. The two pieces cannot proceed simultaneously, and work will not be done faster in this case by assigning several processors to the task.

Even when computations are independent, different stages of a task may require multiple processors to exchange data. In such cases, parallel processing may add some overhead to computations, since some processing time must be allocated to the communication and coordination of the work. In practice, such overhead often means that while the division of work into a few pieces produces a significant gain in the overall speed of a computation, the addition of too many processors may actually impede the work. In dividing a task among machines, there may well be a point when the overhead created by additional processors outweighs any savings obtained by having more processors to do the work, and processors cannot be added to tasks indiscriminately to get the jobs done faster.

═══ RELIABILITY ═══

While speed may be an important issue in designing computer systems, reliability is almost certainly more important. It makes little difference if results are obtained quickly if they are wrong. This need for correct answers is compounded in considering hardware, due to the difficulties of hardware deterioration and failure. Such difficulties suggest two basic questions. First, what are the causes of failure and what can be done to anticipate such problems? Second, given that failures occur, what can be done to detect and correct these problems with minimal disruption? The answers to these questions have a direct bearing on system reliability.

Figure 5-3:   "This time I think it's
                 definitely a hardware problem."

Anticipating Hardware Failure. Many types of hardware failure can
be anticipated through experience. For example, moving parts typically
cause some vibration and heat, and electrical currents generate heat and
electrical fields, and environmental factors may corrode materials. Unfortunately, such vibration and heat cause both electrical connections and
mechanical components to wear and break. Electrical and magnetic fields
can interfere with signals required for controlling equipment. Corrosion
affects materials that make up equipment.

   When such factors are known, they often can be included in product specifications, designs, and maintenance schedules, so that the chance of failure
or damage is minimized. For example, computers are often designed to run
in air conditioned rooms, and ventilation is considered in the design of computer cabinetry. Similarly, dust can seriously interfere with the operation

of computer disk drives, so that air in rooms may be filtered and smoking may be prohibited. Appropriate care in anticipating problems clearly can have a significant impact on system reliability.

As with other types of specifications, however, there is no reason to expect that all such problems can be anticipated. A particularly simple example of this issue motivates the initial use of the term **bug** to refer to an error within a computer. In the early days of computing, when hardware used vacuum tubes and connections were made with a soldering gun, one particular machine had been working fine, when it suddenly started producing unusual results. After some checking, the machine's cabinet was opened, and the nature of the problem became apparent. It seems that an insect (actually a moth) had crawled into the machine and caused a short circuit to occur. The problem was resolved when the electrocuted bug was removed. According to some of today's hardware technicians, similar problems continue to occur, as insects crawl through air conditioning vents and cabinet openings into electrical equipment.

Beyond this historical example, illustrations of unanticipated problems in hardware abound. Near the author's campus, squirrels regularly gnaw through high-voltage electrical lines, causing short circuits and disrupting service. (Due to the voltages and currents involved, however, it is unusual for the same squirrel to cause the same problem twice.) In a more interesting case, on June 11, 1987, the *San Jose Mercury News* reported that three rockets were launched at a NASA facility on Wallops Island, Virginia, due to a lightning strike. It seems that the lightning caused a pulse in current in the leads that activated the rockets' igniters. Other, similar examples of such unanticipated hardware failures are documented regularly in *Software Engineering Notes*.

Such examples illustrate the general principle that one should expect hardware failures to occur. Commenting upon this point, Jan Lee[3] has stated the *Titanic Effect*, which says that "The severity with which a system fails is directly proportional to the intensity of the designer's belief that it cannot." A similar theme is found in a Russian saying, quoted by Herb Lin,[4] concerning the use of rifles on stage in plays, "Once every decade an unloaded gun will fire; once every century a rake will fire." While these notes may be overly cute, they do make a point. If you are sure that failure is impossible, then you are unprepared for anything to happen, and any problems that do occur can cause you to sink. One may not know just what will go wrong within a system, but it is wise to expect that some difficulty will develop.

Once you expect hardware failure to occur, then steps can be made to control the results of failure. Two common approachs to these problems within computer systems involve error correcting codes and redundancy.

Error Correcting Codes. The underlying idea behind error detecting and error correcting codes is illustrated by the following numeric example.

For any number, suppose the sum of the digits is computed, and the units digit of this is recorded. For example, given the number 12645, the sum of the digits is 18 and the units digit of this sum is 8. The number 12645 then may be stored as 12645-8 or 126458. With this computation and storage of an extra digit, simple numeric errors can be detected quite easily. For example, in transmitting 126458 from one machine to another, suppose an error occurred and the number 127458 was received instead. The computer receiving the transmission then could review this number, forming the sum of the digits 1, 2, 7, 4, 5 to get 19 and determining that the units digit here (9) did not match the 8 that was actually received. Thus, the number received could not be correct.

This example outlines a particularly simple way to detect some types of transmission and storage/retrieval errors. Additional data or digits, called **check digits**, may be computed on the basis of the initial data and appended. This approach is one type of **error detecting code**, where data (such as 12645) is encoded into a special form (such as 12645-8), and this new form provides a mechanism for the computer to perform simple checking to determine when some errors have occurred.

This example also shows two difficulties that can arise through the use of error detecting codes. First, while the approach of the example will allow one to detect a single transcription error, where one digit is incorrect, it may not detect other types of errors. For example, this algorithm will not detect the transposition of two digits; an exchange of the 6 and 5 in the number 12645-8 to give 12546-8 will not be found through this checking process. Similarly, errors in two digits may not be detected; writing 12645-8 as 12745-9 still gives a valid number with an appropriate check digit. To resolve these difficulties, two basic approaches typically are followed. Additional check digits may be added, and the computational formulae may involve a variety of different computations. In the previous example, a second check digit might be the sum of the first, third, and fifth digits, so that 12645 might be encoded as 12645-82. (For the second check digit, the sum $1 + 6 + 5$ is computed to get 12, and 2 is recorded.) This approach will detect the transposition of two adjacent digits in a number (why?), but other types of transpositions may not be found. Other formulae may multiply different digits by different values (e.g., the first digit plus 3 times the second digit plus 7 times the third digit plus ...). When each digit is used in a different way, the value of a check digit may be altered when digits are transposed, and transposition errors may be detected.

Second, while a computation of check digits indicates that an error has occurred in the transmission or storage/retrieval of data, error detecting codes do not necessarily allow one to conclude what went wrong. In the example given, 12745-8 can be identified as an incorrect data value, but there is no way to determine that change from the original occurred with the digit 7. Fortunately, with more sophisticated analysis and investigation, formulae can be determined for check digits so that errors cannot only be detected, but the digit(s) in error can be ascertained as well. Such formulae yield **error correcting codes**, which allow both the detection of errors and a determination of where the error occurred. Further, by adding an appropriate number of such digits, it is possible to find and correct as many errors as one wishes. For example, if one wants to anticipate the possibility that two mistakes can occur in the transmission of four-digit numbers, then the addition of three check digits allow not only the testing for up to two transmission errors but also the correction of zero, one, or two such problems. If more digits are added, then even more mistakes can be found and corrected.

In practice, the use of error detecting and correcting codes resolves a very large percentage of the problems that might arise within computers with regard to the storage/retrieval and transmission of data. For example, in the sending of data from one machine to another, error detecting codes normally are used to check each piece of data sent. When errors are found, the data may be retransmitted. Similarly, error detecting codes normally are used when values are stored on a disk. Here, invalid data can be identified when they are read, but the correct values may not be known. In such cases, errors may be reported to computer users, but it may or may not be realistic to determine what the correct values should be. Within machines themselves, both error detecting and correcting codes may be used. In such cases, values may be corrected as mistakes are found, and processing can continue without further delay. In practice, these codes are used heavily, and it is quite rare (but not impossible, of course) for data to be corrupted by hardware. Problems normally are routinely reported automatically when they are detected, so it is quite unlikely that hardware malfunctions will arise without the user knowing about them.

Redundancy. The second common method to allow computing to continue following some hardware (or software) malfunctions involves the notion of redundancy. The basic idea is illustrated rather simply by students who regularly bring two pencils or two pens to a test. There is always the chance that a pencil point will break or a pen will run out of ink, and such an occurrence can have a serious impact upon a person's performance on the exercise. With two writing implements, one can serve as a spare if the other breaks or runs out of ink.

System Redundancy – More generally, redundancy involves allowing two or more pieces of hardware or software to perform a task in parallel. If one piece malfunctions, then the remaining equipment or programs can take over without disruption. For example, a computer system may be equipped with two disk drives to store identical data, and normally each copy of this information is updated whenever changes are made. Check digits are used to verify the correctness of data each time they are read, and in the absence of errors, either drive may be used. When errors are detected in check digits from one drive, however, then the data from the other drive may be used, assuming the check digits for this second copy of data are correct. With this duplication of data, processing can continue when one disk drive malfunctions, since errors can be detected and a backup copy utilized. Overall processing must halt only if both disk drives malfunction.

With redundant systems, then, processing can continue as long as some equipment and software works correctly. Multiple failures are required before the entire system must stop, and normally it seems reasonable to expect that the failure of one system will not imply the failure of another system. For example, when a bearing wears out in one drive, it seems unlikely that a different bearing in another drive would wear out at the same time. Both of these are mechanical devices, and one would not expect wear to affect parts in different machines in exactly the same way. Such a situation illustrates the notion of **independence**, where the proper functioning of one machine or computer program does not affect the operation of another. Thus, one might expect that multiple disk drives will work independently, since a mechanical failure for one drive is unlikely to affect the second drive.

This independence of operation seems to apply to many circumstances, and redundant systems can be useful in many applications. In the case of using two pens, it seems unlikely that both will run out of ink at the same time. Similarly, breaking one pencil point does not seem to imply that another pencil point will break. This suggests that carrying two pens or pencils can be particularly helpful in guarding against running out of ink or breaking a point.

This writing example, however, also illustrates a basic question that one must always consider whenever redundancy is used. In particular, how can one be certain that two systems or pieces of equipment or writing implements do function independently? For writing implements, for example, suppose that two pencils may be kept in the same carrying case. Then both points may be broken if the case drops. Similarly, two pens kept together may be destroyed if the pen container is run over by the family car. On a less dramatic level, if you regularly alternate your use of pens, then the ink supply of each will be depleted at about the same rate, and they may become dry at about the same time. In this context, it may be safer to have one pencil and one pen, so that different types of failure are needed before both implements are unusable. Similarly, it might be better to carry the two writing implements in separate places, so the dropping or destruction of one will not also affect the other. Redundancy can be very helpful in resolving problems related to failure, but care is needed to reduce the likelihood that several systems will fail at once.

In practice, maintaining the independence of systems or components can be quite difficult. For example, if two separate disk drives are connected to the same electrical circuit, then both will become disabled when the same circuit breaker is tripped. A short circuit in one drive, therefore, may trigger the breaker that halts the other drive. Similarly, separate machines may be connected by several separate wires to provide independent communication paths. If these wires physically belong to a single cable, however, then a single cut of the cable (perhaps by a bulldozer excavating a site containing underground cables miles from the computing equipment) could disrupt all of the separate communication lines.

At a more subtle level, two disk drives or other devices from the same manufacturer may share a common defect, so that when that defect disrupts the operation of one drive it is likely to affect the other drive as well. (For example, a bearing might be likely to give out above a certain temperature. Then, when the temperature rises, this same problem might reasonably arise in all drives containing that type of bearing.) As a second example, when returning to earth on April 19, 1985, one of the main wheel sets of the shuttle *Discovery* locked and then another, blowing out one tire and shredding another. Here, redundant tires were part of the design, but both tires failed at the same time.[5]

When systems are particularly critical and hardware malfunctions could be disastrous, there is a special need to avoid the possibility of common defects or problems arising in multiple systems. In such cases, redundancy can be obtained by using different designs, algorithms, and hardware. When two systems use different equipment and controlling software, common problems may seem particularly unlikely.[6]

Algorithms – While duplication of systems achieves one form of redundancy, such systems must simultaneously fail if they contain the same flaws. For example, if a system contains a logic error in its controlling software, then every copy of that system will be guided by the same error, and all can be expected to produce identical, but wrong, results. To address such difficulties, one approach is to develop systems independently to perform the same task. For example, separate designs and algorithms may be developed and different programs written for different computers. With different teams working on different equipment, it seems particularly unlikely that errors made by one group will also be made by another group. Two programs written by different people following distinct approaches to a problem will have little in common, and the likelihood of dependencies between systems is decreased.

The following report, however, shows that even multiple redundancies cannot assure correct functioning.

> During the development of the Handley Page Victor jet bomber, roughly a contemporary of the B-52, the designers were concerned about possible problems with the unusual tailplane design. They were particularly worried about "flutter" – a positive feedback loop between slightly-flexible structures and the airflow around them, [which is] dangerous when the frequency of the resulting oscillation matches a resonant frequency of the structure. So they tested for tailplane flutter very carefully:
>
> 1. A specially-built wind-tunnel model was used to investigate the flutter behavior. (Because one cannot scale down the fluid properties of the atmosphere, a simple scale model of the aircraft isn't good enough to check on subtle problems – the model must be carefully built to answer a specific question.)
>
> 2. Resonance tests were run on the first prototype before it flew, with the results cranked into aerodynamic equations.
>
> 3. Early flight tests included some tests whose results could be extrapolated to reveal flutter behavior. (Flutter is sensitive to speed, so low-speed tests could be run safely.)
>
> All three methods produced similar answers, agreeing that there was no flutter problem in the tailplane at any speed the aircraft could reach.
>
> Somewhat later, when the first prototype was doing high-speed low-altitude passes over an airbase for instrument calibration, the tailplane broke off. The aircraft crashed instantly, killing the entire crew. A long investigation finally discovered what happened:
>
> 1. The stiffness of a crucial part in the wind-tunnel flutter model was wrong.
>
> 2. One term in the aerodynamic equations had been put in wrongly.
>
> 3. The flight-test results involved some tricky problems of data interpretation, and the engineers had been misled.
>
> And by sheer bad luck, all three wrong answers were roughly the same number.[7]

Beyond this possibility that separate algorithms will produce the same incorrect results, three additional issues can affect one's confidence in the correctness of redundant systems. First, any design, algorithm, software package, or hardware depends ultimately upon the specifications that are stated for the problem. Systems may work independently and correctly following the same specifications. When specifications contain errors, however, this would only ensure that all systems would produce the same invalid results. Redundant systems cannot make up for mistakes in specifications.

Second, any system is dependent upon the data it receives during processing. (The commonly used acronym is *GIGO* – garbage in, garbage out.) When people enter information into a computer system, typographical errors are always possible. When sensors are attached to computer systems to give information on temperature, velocity, radar signals, and so forth, there is always the possibility that a sensor may malfunction, giving incorrect data to all machines attached to it. In either of these situations, computers may respond correctly to the information they have, but the basic data may be in error. If the same data are distributed to redundant systems, then all machines will base results upon the same, incorrect information, and all can be expected to reach the same erroneous conclusions.

Third, more subtle problems arise when determining how to proceed when redundant systems produce conflicting conclusions.

Conflict Resolution – When redundant systems control a single machine or operation, then all processing must result in a single course of action. For example, several computers may monitor the flight of a plane or rocket, but only one set of signals can be sent to direct the aircraft's movement. (Clearly, the controls for the left side of the aircraft cannot instruct a plane to prepare for landing at the same time the right side controls direct the plane to ascend 5,000 feet.) With redundant computer systems, however, it is possible that different machines will reach distinct, conflicting conclusions. In such cases, some mechanism must be devised to resolve the conflict; some approach is needed to decide which system is correct or which should be ignored.

When several (at least three) separate systems are used, one simple approach may be called **majority rule**. Each system reports its conclusions, and the answer supported by the majority of the systems is used for subsequent action. Such an approach, for example, was used in the space shuttle Orbiter.[8] In this scheme, the system was designed to use four computers. If any one gave results that differed from the others, then that system could be shut down, and operations could continue with three. Then, if a second failure occurred, the two machines working properly would still have a majority vote over the malfunctioning machine. Thus, with four machines, failures could occur in two systems and the two remaining systems would still be able to provide correct, consistent information for controlling the spacecraft's flight. (More discussion of the Orbiter's system may be found in Chapter 6.)

A second approach presents the results from redundant systems to a pilot, human operator, or other arbitrator, who then determines how to proceed.

With conflicting data, the arbitrator may request additional information or consider other factors before deciding which course of action to follow. Such an approach involves a time delay while the arbitrator is resolving the causes for an inconsistency, but this approach does allow more information to be gathered and additional checks to be made. Ultimately, even with this approach, however, some choice must be made as to which system(s) are malfunctioning and which are providing appropriate information.

Complexity – While adding redundancy to systems can allow for the detection and appropriate handling of a variety of hardware and software errors, redundancy is not without cost. Multiple systems clearly require additional hardware, power, space, and other resources. In addition, redundant systems often must use complex logic to tie components together. For example, redundant systems often share data from the same sensors or disk drives or keyboards, so mechanisms must be developed to allow the same data to be communicated to different machines. In addition, multiple systems frequently must communicate with each other. For example, in a majority rule approach to conflict resolution, systems must send data to each other so that results can be compared. A malfunctioning system may need to shut itself down, and other systems must know which machines are functioning properly and which machines are authorized to operate what controls. In such an environment, communications among systems is essential, but such communications logic can greatly increase the complexity the operation of each individual system. Such an increase in complexity naturally increases the likelihood that errors will be made in designing and building a system. Chapter 6, for example, describes the complexity added to the Orbiter's software due to redundancy which led to a system shut down and a delayed launch.

Overall, then, redundancy can help increase the likelihood of detecting some types of errors and in guarding against hardware and software failures. This can help systems to function smoothly, even when some components fail. On the other hand, redundancy increases the cost and the complexity of systems, and redundant systems may contain more logical errors than simplier ones.

═ SUMMARY ═

1. Modern techniques allow the design and construction of much hardware to proceed efficiently and effectively with relatively few errors. Much computer hardware itself is based on a few, well understood basic circuits, and large, sophisticated computer chips are constructed from hundreds or thousands of these circuits.

- Computer-assisted design (CAD) systems allow the checking and analysis of circuits in complex chip designs within the design stage.

- Verification techniques provide formal, mathematical analysis of circuit designs, and these techniques allow designers to prove logically that specific plans will meet desired specifications for computer hardware.

2. While the history of computing is marked by remarkable increases in the speed of processing, further progress must respect two basic limitations:

   - Data cannot move through computers at speeds exceeding the speed of light, since this determines the speed of electricity as well. Since different computer components are physically separated, the speed of light limits how fast data can flow between components. Similar issues limit how fast data can flow within a single component.

   - Miniaturization of components and circuits is limited by the size of atoms and molecules. Circuits cannot be smaller than molecular size.

   With the impressive speed and size of today's machines, each of these factors proves that the current pace of increasing speed and power of machines cannot continue indefinitely.

3. While individual chips or machines may be limited in their speed and size, the use of parallelism has the potential to increase the speed and capability of some types of computations. Work in individual computations may not be improved, but many separate and independent computations may be performed simultaneously.

4. All hardware suffers from the possibility of mechanical or electrical malfunctions; hardware can wear out.

5. Some types of hardware failure can be anticipated, and preventive maintenance can be designed so that parts normally are replaced or serviced before they wear out or fail.

6. Other types of failure cannot be anticipated. For example, lightning strikes, power surges, and plumbing leaks may occur with little or no warning. One cannot expect problems from such causes to be prevented by a regular maintenance schedule.

7. Systems can be built to anticipate, detect, and sometimes resolve failures. Error detecting and correcting codes use check digits to provide a built-in check of all data stored in a system. Redundancy may allow several components to check each other's results.

8. While redundancy can help detect errors, this approach also introduces two additional issues. First, mechanisms must be developed to resolve conflicts when different machines produce conflicting results. Second, redundancy often increases the complexity of equipment considerably, and increased complexity may introduce new opportunities for error within a system.

═══ CONCLUSIONS AND IMPLICATIONS ═══

Computer hardware normally is comprised of many simple circuits, and this has enabled the process for developing hardware to be refined to an impressive level. Modern techniques and practices allow many types of hardware to be developed effectively and efficiently to perform tasks required in specifications. Innovations in testing and verification can provide assurances that hardware will function in the way it was intended. When these approaches are followed, one can have a reasonably high level of confidence that newly manufactured hardware will meet desired specifications.

Unfortunately, mechanical and electrical equipment wear out. When failures can be anticipated, preventive maintenance often can replace components before they fail, and machines can run reliably for long periods of time. On the other hand, unanticipated events can have a serious impact upon systems, and there is no way to anticipate all possible difficulties that might occur. Such chance occurrences can have a particularly significant impact upon system reliability.

Techniques, such as error detecting and correcting codes and redundancy, can help systems identify when errors occur and possibly continue functioning in spite of component failures. Unfortunately, redundancy can also have the effect of adding considerably to system complexity, which can introduce new types of errors.

Overall, hardware is subject to a variety of failures, both anticipated and unanticipated, but many of these difficulties can be anticipated, detected, and corrected. Hardware, therefore, can be a very reliable part of many systems. With sufficient care in development, mistakes in designs can be eliminated, and problems due to component failure can be identified and resolved. To a large degree, hardware is simpler and better understood than software and various human–computer interactions. Limitations may arise in issues of speed and logical complexity, but in many cases, hardware can be expected to behave reliably in complex systems.

═══ **DISCUSSION QUESTIONS** ═══

5.1 Assuming that hardware does wear out, what dangers are inherent in systems built to run on hardware platforms when replacement parts are not available? Have you experienced such difficulties? When does hardware become too old? What types of components have you observed getting old first?

5.2 The anecdote at the beginning of this chapter describes a rather unorthodox way in which one intermittent hardware problem was identified and solved. Does this story have any broader implications? Does it help identify any principles concerning hardware? Explain your answer.

5.3 This chapter presents some statistics about how far data can travel in a second, even at the speed of light. While distances are continually being decreased within computers, one clear minimum involves the size of molecules. The size of a typical molecule is roughly six to ten angstroms (i. e., between 6×10^{-8} and 10×10^{-8} centimeters or approximately 3×10^{-8} inches), and in any storage medium, two storage cells would be separated by at least one molecule.

   a. Assuming information could move at the speed of light, what is the theoretical minimum for moving a piece of data from one storage cell to another? (In this problem, you can ignore details of how one cell will know to send or record the new piece of information – consider only issues of moving data from one place to another.)

   b. Suppose main memory were to contain one million cells of storage, packed together in a 100-by-100-by-100 rectangular grid. What is the minimum time possible for a piece of data to be moved from any cell to any other one? (As with part (a), consider only the time required to move data.)

5.4 This chapter mentions several times that environmental factors, such as vibration and heat, can cause equipment to deteriorate, and a few causes of these factors are identified at a general level.

   a. What do you think might be major sources of such vibration and heat in computing equipment?

   b. Can you identify some devices that might be more likely to have difficulties due to vibration than others?

   c. Can you think of ways that problems of vibration and heat could be minimized?

5.5   It is widely observed that equipment with moving parts, such as disk drives and printers, has a much higher failure rate than equipment that is completely electrical. Explain why one might expect this failure pattern.

5.6   It has been said that in 1969 a mechanic would have needed to read 5,000 pages of manuals in order to repair any car available on the market. By 1990, the requisite number of pages would be 500,000.

a. How much has computerization contributed to this?

b. Are similar problems appearing in the fields of hardware or software maintenance?

NOTES

1   According to some sources, this success rate in developing chips has had a noticeable effect upon the jewelry market. For some years, it has been fashionable (at least in some circles) to wear jewelry (e.g., ear rings, cuff links, tie tacks) made from computer chips. In the past, this jewelry often could be made from early chip prototypes that failed to meet their specifications. These defective chips did not do the task required of them, but they still looked nice in jewelry. Further, since the chip design process was very complex and error prone, large numbers of defective chips were available whenever a new chip was being developed. Today, many laboratories develop new chips with very few initial mistakes, reducing this source of supply for jewelry considerably. Thus, today it is not unknown for functioning chips to be sacrificed for jewelry, since defective ones are not always available.

2   The Theory of Relativity from physics implies that the speed of light gives an upper bound on the speed of any communication between points. However, the actual speeds for many types of transmission are only a fraction of the speed of light. For example, evidence suggests that electrical impulses traveling through coaxial cable may travel at only about two-thirds the speed of light. One possible approach for increasing the speed of computers, therefore, is to use light (moving in a vacuum) rather than electrical impulses (traveling through wires) for transmitting data from one point to another. Such innovative approaches could allow a significant increase in computer processing speed, but even these new machines would be limited by the speed of light.

As an aside, it is interesting to note that electrons traveling through a wire travel much more slowly than this theoretical maximum. The actual speed of electrons depends upon the amount of current in the circuit and various characteristics of the medium conducting the current. For example, a current of 1 ampere travels through a copper wire with a diameter of 1 millimeter at the rate of 4.69×10^{-3} centimeters per second. Such speeds are typical of many types of circuits. On the other hand, in sending an impulse, one electron may "push" the electrons ahead of it, and the electrical pulse therefore moves dramatically faster than the electron itself.

3   *Software Engineering Notes*, Volume 11, Number 1, January 1986, p. 14.

4   *Software Engineering Notes*, Volume 11, Number 1, January 1986, p. 14.

5   In fact, this difficulty was anticipated three years earlier, in January 1982, when the Aerospace Safety Advisory Panel noted the "design is such that should a tire fail, its mate (almost certainly) would also fail - a potential hazard," but this and other warnings were ignored. For more information, see *Science*, 3 May 1985, p. 562, and *Software Engineering Notes*, Volume 10, Number 3, July 1985, p. 10.

6   While systems use different designs, equipment, and software often in independent ways, the reader may want to read on before reaching any final conclusions.

7   Reported in *Software Engineering Notes*, Volume 11, Number 2, April 1986, p. 12, corrected by *Software Engineering Notes*, Volume 11, Number 3, July 1986, p. 25. For further reference, see Bill Gunston, "Bombers of the West," Scribner, New York, 1973.

8   Reported by John R. Garman, "The "Bug" Heard 'Round the World," *Software Engineering Notes*, Volume 6, Number 5, October 1981, p. 3.

PART IV
Software

"It goes on to say, 'The fault isn't with the hardware. It's with you—the software' "

Software provides the controls and directions that the hardware carries out. From one perspective, the role of hardware is reasonably straightforward. Hardware must be able to store and retrieve data, move data from place to place, perform simple arithmetic operations on data (e.g., addition, subtraction, multiplication, division), and compare two pieces of data. While the design of hardware to perform these tasks efficiently requires considerable background in electronics, each function is simple and well understood. Hardware development, therefore, is a reasonably restricted and well defined field.

From this same perspective, one might argue that software involves everything else in computing beyond hardware. While such a definition may be a bit too broad, this view does suggest the range and complexity of issues that legitimately arise under the general heading of "software."

This part explores some of this breadth by considering various characteristics and issues related to software. Since software tells a machine what to do, errors in instructions to hardware may yield incorrect or undesired results. Chapter 6 reviews some types of software errors and concludes with some observations on the cost of writing correct programs. Chapter 7 then focuses on a particular type of software, namely software that runs simulations. While simulations can be a very powerful technique in studying complex phenomena, simulation programs are also prone to many of the same problems that affect other types of software as well.

In Chapter 8, the focus shifts to human factors that affect the correct functioning of computers and programs. Since human error is always potentially present in the running of a computer system, software often includes various tests to help identify mistakes made by computer operators or users. While these checks can catch errors quickly, provisions also must be made for the possiblity that software itself contains errors. Such opportunities for error give rise to a tension between capabilities provided to users and those reserved for software.

In Chapter 9, the discussion turns to issues of computer security. Here, the basic concern is preventing unauthorized access of data and programs within a computer system. As in Chapter 8, software can help monitor many potential security problems. On the other hand, weaknesses in software can also be exploited in accessing sensitive data.

CHAPTER 6

Murphy's First Law:
 Anything that can go wrong will.

Observation:
 Murphy was an optimist.

Program Correctness

Already, previous chapters have identified difficulties that are inherent with stating problems. Additional difficulties arise when specifications are determined. Some problems are unsolvable, while solutions to some others take too long in all but the most trivial cases. In spite of these limitations, this chapter begins by assuming that both appropriate specifications for a problem and feasible solutions have been found. With these optimistic assumptions, the chapter considers the likelihood that finished software packages will meet their specifications. The basic question addressed is, "To what extent can one expect programs to meet the needs of the problems they are meant to solve?"

To address this question, this chapter first considers what can go wrong when specifications or algorithms are translated into a form for use in computers. Algorithms may be known in an abstract form, but work is still required to formulate or program these algorithms so that they will run on particular machines. When this work is complex, there are many opportunities for error,[1] and people have found many creative ways to make mistakes.

Next, when errors are made, the chapter discusses the likelihood that those errors will be found. If tests or simulations or other techniques allow all errors to be found and corrected, then the quality of software would improve over time and progressively more confidence might be placed in its functioning. On the other hand, if it is unlikely that all errors have been found, then it might seem risky to place much trust in the proper working of the programs. Similarly, confidence in programs can be undermined if errors cannot be corrected once they are identified. In some cases, processing may proceed by working around known errors, but there may always be some question about the reliability of software which is known to be incorrect in some cases.

In some ways, one could regard this discussion of possible errors as the work of a pessimist; many things do work reasonably well in spite of Murphy's Law. The track record for software, however, does not foster confidence, and this chapter illustrates its discussion with a wide range of actual examples. Errors abound in many computer programs, and history suggests that real programs of any size always contain errors. (In some programs that have been in use for several years, past errors sometimes are even advertised as being "features.") This suggests that there may be some reason to believe the observation about Murphy.

═══ **THE BASIS FOR IDENTIFYING ERRORS** ═══

Chapter 1 observed that the problem-solving process involves several basic steps. From the perspective of this chapter, it is useful to group these steps into three categories:

- formulating specifications,

- using specifications to develop computer programs, and

- maintaining programs.

The first two of these categories involve the solution of a problem from the first vague vision of what is to be done to the completion of a formal computer program that solves the problem. The remaining category involves modification of programs to meet new needs or to correct past difficulties.

In considering these distinct categories, any actual programs then can be evaluated from several perspectives. Ultimately, the value of a program depends upon whether it is helpful in solving the actual problem under consideration. Programs are useful only if they meet the needs of the people responsible for solving specific tasks. (Even if programs meet their specifications and give correct answers, they may have little value if they are too cumbersome to use or if they produce results in a form that is not helpful to people doing a job.) Formally, the evaluation of programs from this perspective of the actual problem is called **program validation**; program validation includes a program giving correct, helpful answers in a form that people can use as they perform their work. From a more limited perspective, programs can also be evaluated as to whether they meet the specifications formulated for the problem, and this type of evaluation is called **program verification**. In a perfect world, specifications are correct and complete, and then validation and verification are equivalent. Any difficulty in solving the actual problem may be translated into a difficulty in a program meeting its specifications.

Chapter 2, however, has argued that it is often impossible to know if specifications are correct and complete, particularly when problems are complex. Specifications may contain errors, omit important details, or contain inconsistencies. In such cases, computer programs may meet given specifications, but the programs still may not be very helpful in handling the original problem. On the other hand, when a program does not meet the stated specifications, it is possible that the mistake in the program is counterbalanced by a mistake in the specifications and the program works correctly for the actual problem.[2] While such a cancellation of errors theoretically is possible, in practice such luck almost never happens. Normally, errors that cause programs to violate their specifications also produce incorrect results in the actual problem. When specifications are wrong, however, it is possible that programs can be verified as meeting their specifications while failing to meet validation tests. Programs may not be helpful in solving actual problems even when they meet all of their specifications in great detail.

Once programs are written for one problem, it is common for modifications to be necessary. For example, changes in legal requirements, the emergence of new accounting practices, or experience with existing computer systems all may lead to a need to modify programs to meet new needs. More generally, demands for new capabilities or needs for revised processing practices may be viewed as changing both the actual problem to be solved and the formal specifications. In this context, validation and verification both refer to revised problems, and programs often must be rewritten or modified to respond to these changes. When programs are large, it is rarely practical to rewrite them completely, and program modification is often the only viable way to proceed. While such changes often provide the user of a program with new capabilities, these changes also often introduce errors into parts of the program that worked well previously. As with the writing of original programs, the final evaluation of programs depends upon the actual problem to be solved. With modifications, however, programs may fail to work as required, even when they worked correctly in the past.

═══ WHERE ERRORS COME FROM ═══

One of the sad truths of human nature is that people can be extremely resourceful and imaginative in finding new ways to make mistakes. In a religious context, one might view this observation from an abstract philosophical perspective, perhaps discussing the concept of original sin. In this book, however, the view is much more practical, and this section addresses some important factors that can lead to errors in the development of software. With many such factors identified, the question arises as to whether it is possible to produce error-free software in the future.

Already the discussion of specifications in Chapter 2 observed that some errors may arise from omissions and inconsistencies in the specifications for a problem. Similar issues can arise in writing code. In addition, algorithm development and programming may include other types of errors, including rounding and numerical errors and typographical errors. Further errors can arise when several machines are connected into a network. The following discussion considers each of these types of errors in some detail.

Omissions and Inconsistencies. As discussed in Chapter 2, one of the most common sources of errors in programs involves omissions and inconsistencies. Particularly in large, complex systems, small or simple tasks are easily forgotten. In some cases, such difficulties may depend upon oversights in specifications, but in other cases errors may be due to the code itself. The following examples illustrate possible consequences that may arise from these omissions and inconsistencies.

Example: WWMCCS[3] – The World Wide Military Command and Control System is a computer network designed to provide communications for the military both in peace time and during emergencies. In November 1978, a power failure disrupted communications between Florida and Washington, D.C. When power was restored, however, the Washington computer was unable to re-establish communication with the Florida machine. In reviewing the specifications, it seems that mechanisms were available for connecting new machines to the existing systems, and additional computers could "log on" to the network. However, no one had anticipated the need for an existing computer to log on to the system a second time, and this omission prevented the computers from re-establishing communications in a normal manner following the blackout.

Example: ABM Defense System[4] – Since computers are used to control the launch of rockets in the Anti-Ballistic Missile (ABM) defense system of the United States, officers must be trained in operating these rockets appropriately. Due to the expense of such systems, it has been proposed that the same computers be used for both the training of personnel and the actual firing of ABMs. In one scenario, the actions of officers would be the same for training as for actual launch, although in a training exercise a statement at the top of the screen would indicate that missiles would not actually be fired. Borenstein has noted, however, that in such situations a simple programming error could result in the failure of the training message to be erased, leading an officer to believe that a launch sequence was part of a training simulation instead of the countdown to an actual launch. Here, the omission of one line in a program of thousands of lines could result in the accidental launching of missiles during a simple training exercise.

Such examples indicate that omissions and inconsistencies in specifications may have considerable consequences when programs are actually used. Additional errors may arise due to simple omissions in designing algorithms and in writing programs themselves. Each step of the problem-solving process is open to errors, and an error at any stage can have significant results.

Round-off/Numerical Errors. Two rather different types of error can arise when numbers are processed in computers. Each of these errors depends upon how numbers are stored, retrieved, and printed and upon how numerical operations are performed.

Within computers, most numbers are stored either as integers (positive or negative whole numbers or zero) or as real numbers (numbers with decimal points). For example, integers include -1234 and 56 and 32767, while real numbers include −37.5 and 1234.75 and 0.0000056. It is not impossible to handle other types of numbers, but such storage is relatively uncommon. For example, fractions are sometimes handled by storing both a numerator and a denominator that are integers, while complex numbers may be handled by storing two real numbers (a real and imaginary part). These expanded numbers, however, still usually depend upon standard integers or real numbers, and issues applying to integers and real numbers, therefore, also apply to most other types as well.

In a computer, integers are stored exactly, although technically the numbers are represented in the binary system (or base 2) rather than in the more familiar decimal (or base 10) system. In this representation, the values are kept exactly, and arithmetic operations such as addition and subtraction produce exact results in most common cases.

Storage limitations for integers arise, however, due to storage constraints within machines. In particular, storage space in computers is finite, and designers of computers therefore must make decisions about how to allocate this space. Such decisions inevitably restrict the size allowed for integers. For example, in computers called 16-bit machines, integers normally are restricted to the range −32,768 to 32,767. (Technically, this range depends upon 16 binary (or base 2) digits, and the numbers must be between -2^{15} and $2^{15} - 1$.) In more powerful 32-bit microcomputers, integers are still restricted, but the range is expanded to −2,147,483,648 to 2,147,483,647 (or -2^{31} to $2^{31} - 1$). Arithmetic operations producing integer results within this range are also exact. For many applications this range of integers is quite adequate, and these computer limitations do not pose difficulties.

Outside of these ranges arithmetic operations can produce results that are not intended. For example, on a 16-bit machine where the maximum integer is 32,767, the addition 32,765 + 5 will go outside the limits of the computer. This condition is called **overflow**, and the computer must interpret the result in some way. Sometimes, a computer is programmed to print an error message when overflow occurs, and further processing may cease. In other cases, the computer may interpret the result in some undesired way (perhaps considering the result of 32,765 + 5 as −32,766) and continuing processing. Details will depend upon the particular computer and application, but users should understand that such difficulties are always possible.

More severe limitations arise in working with real numbers (numbers with decimal points). To introduce these problems, consider the decimal representation of the fraction 1/3. By long division,

$$1/3 \ = \ 0.3333333333333333333333333\ldots$$

and this sequence of 3's continues forever. Computers, however, are finite, so they cannot store such a sequence exactly. Instead, real numbers in computers must be truncated (or rounded) after some number of digits. For example, if a computer stored seven significant digits of accuracy, then for the computer 1/3 is exactly 0.3333333.

Beyond this simple example, applications typically require computers to handle extremely large real numbers, such as 2.464987×10^{23}, and numbers very close to zero, such as 6.06754×10^{-18}. With these demands, storage of real numbers represents a compromise between the need for accuracy and the need to handle a wide range of values. In order to meet these needs, storage of real numbers usually involves the following general steps: (Actually, real numbers are stored using the binary system rather than the decimal system, but the following ideas apply to either system.)

1. A number is written in an exponential or "scientific" notation. For example, 123,456,789,012,345 would be written as $1.23456789012345 \times 10^{14}$, while 0.000000013256 would be written as 1.3256×10^{-8}. More generally, this results in a number of the form $a \times 10^{b}$, where a is called the **mantissa** and b is called the **exponent**. Normally in this form, a has exactly one digit before the decimal point, and b may be either a positive or a negative integer.

2. Once a number is written in exponential form, then the mantissa is truncated, if necessary, to a specified number of digits. For example, if seven digits are allocated for a mantissa, then $1.23456789012345 \times 10^{14}$ would be revised to read 1.234567×10^{14}, while no revision is needed for the five-digit mantissa in 1.3256×10^{-8}.

3. With this revision, both the mantissa and the exponent are stored. For example, for 1.234567×10^{14}, both numbers 1.234567 and 14 are stored, while for 1.3256×10^{-8}, the numbers 1.3256 and -8 are recorded.

As with integers, this storage of real numbers works well for many applications, although sometimes side effects can be rather troublesome. For example, if seven digits of accuracy are maintained, then as noted previously, $(1/3) \ = \ 0.3333333$, so $3 \times (1/3) \ = \ 3 \times 0.3333333 \ = \ 0.9999999$. While this number is close to 1, it is no longer the case that $3 \times (1/3)$ will be considered as exactly 1.

As another example, consider what happens when a large number is added to a small one. For example, suppose 1 is added to 12,345,670 (or 1.234567×10^{7}). Here, one would like the result to be 12,345,671, but the number of digits in this mantissa exceeds what can be stored. The result, therefore, must be truncated back to 7 digits, and 12,345,670 + 1 = 12,345,670 . The large number is not changed in any way by adding a small number. Similarly, 1 could be added 1,000 times to 12,345,670, and in each case the result would be the same starting number. In contrast, adding 1,000 directly to 12,345,670 would give the expected result of 12,346,670. Hence, if the thousand 1's were added first to each other to get 1,000 and this result were added to 12,345,670, then the overall sum would change. If each 1 were added to the large number separately, however, no change would result. This result is quite different than one might expect from mathematics, where the order of arithmetic does not matter. In computers, the order of addition may affect the answer obtained.

An even more dramatic effect may be seen when two numbers of similar sizes are subtracted. For example,[5] consider the simple subtraction problem 12,345,679 − 12,345,670, where one would hope the result would be 9. If computers only store real numbers to seven digits, then both of these numbers might be truncated to 1.234567×10^7 and their difference would be 0.

Each of these examples demonstrates that the storage of real numbers frequently can introduce inaccuracies into computations, and such inaccuracies can be compounded when computations are performed. Additional analysis shows that even simple errors can grow to be quite large when many steps and operations are necessary in a complex computation. Results can be changed dramatically if small errors are allowed to grow through hundreds or thousands of computations. In some cases, the errors may be larger than the desired results themselves.

This observation illustrates the first type of numerical error that can arise in computing systems. Inaccuracies in the measurement or storage of real numbers can be compounded with extensive processing. Such errors can have a significant effect on results that are obtained. The following two examples illustrate this difficulty further.

Example: Designing Aircraft[6] **–** In designing aircraft, one computation required the computation of the sine of a 20-digit number. In this computation, the normal approach is to subtract multiples of π to obtain a result between 0 and 2π and then apply the sine function. In this particular case, however, the computer used for the computation only stored 20 digits of accuracy. Thus, after the initial subtraction, no digits of accuracy remained, just as in the previous, simpler example. The result of the subtraction was completely meaningless. Thus, the sine function was applied to an essentially random number, and the result was used to design aircraft.

Example: The Vancouver Stock Exchange Index – Between 1981 and 1983, the Vancouver Stock Exchange Index was computed with each trade of stock, using four decimal places in the computation, but the result was then truncated (not rounded) to three places of accuracy. This computation was then repeated with each of the approximately 3000 trades that occur daily. As a result of the truncation of the calculation to three decimal places, the index lost about 1 point a day, or about 20 points per month. Thus, to correct this consistent numerical error, the Index was recomputed and corrected over the weekend of November 26, 1983. Specifically, when trading concluded on November 25, the Vancouver Stock Exchange Index was quoted as 524.811, while the corrected figure used to open on Monday morning was 1098.892. Here the correction for 22 months of compounded error caused the Index to raise 574.081 over a weekend without any changes in stock prices. In each of these cases, computations began with correct data but subsequent processing introduced a significant error into the results.

A second type of difficulty encountered with real numbers can arise when users place undue significance on the accuracy of the results obtained. In some cases, this problem arises when users expect the results of a computation to be more accurate than the data entered. For example, temperatures for a month may be recorded, based on a simple thermometer that gives readings to the nearest degree. Thus, in the summer, high readings might be 89, 93, 95, 94, 98, 96, 91. Each of these readings is correct only to the nearest whole number, but the user might ask for five decimal places in an average to get 93.71429. In such a computation, the last several digits have no significance whatsoever, since the initial numbers each could be off by half a degree or so. Here computers will respond with any number of digits desired, but people must use some judgement in interpreting the results.

As another example, at one college an honor society uses students' grade point averages (GPAs) to determine who will be invited to join the group. Since such averages are based on specific grades, each GPA may be computed exactly, but there may be limits concerning differences that are considered significant. One year, in the election process, GPAs for a class were computed to two decimal places, candidates for the society were ordered by this computation, and the society members looked at the list to find an appropriate break point. Specifically, it was decided that the list would be scanned, and those grouped closely together at the top of the list would be inducted. When a large enough gap was found between this top group and the next person on the list, then no more people would be considered. This scheme seemed reasonable to the society's current membership, and a proposed gap was found. (While specific details may differ somewhat for that list, GPAs appeared, roughly, as ... , 3.61, 3.60, 3.58, 3.57, ... , and the "large gap" of 0.02 between 3.60 and 3.58 seemed twice as large as the 0.01 found between the other scores.) When the same data were used to recompute GPAs to 3 decimal places, however, and the sequence went ... , 3.608, 3.596, 3.584, 3.566, ... , showing a gap of 0.012 between the first three GPAs, and then a larger jump of 0.018 before the last score. This computation showed that the position of the "large gap" depended upon whether GPAs were computed to two or three decimal places. Subsequently, the question was raised as to whether such minor differences from one GPA to another were a valid way to distinguish between students, or whether other approaches to evaluation might be more appropriate. Here the computer could produce results to any reasonable level of accuracy based upon exact data, but it was not clear that fine distinctions had any real significance.

Overall, these examples show that the computer is able to perform many computations very quickly, but care is always needed in interpreting the results. In some cases, storage of numbers in the computer may introduce some inaccuracies. Then computations, particularly subtraction, may compound errors already present. Finally, the computer may be asked to print answers involving either more or less accuracy than is appropriate. When important decisions depend upon the accuracy of any answers, it is necessary to analyze how accurate any final results might be. Without a careful analysis, results from a computation must be used with some caution.

Typographical Errors. While omissions, inconsistencies, and numerical errors often reflect subtleties in a problem or an algorithm, a much more elementary difficulty can involve typographical errors. Computer programs give instructions to computers just as English phrases and sentences may instruct people. On computer programs, many such errors are identified by the computer itself, for some typographical errors can make a program unintelligible. As an analogy, if you receive a statement "o7hdy w5q45w q5 9h3 5y8456," you immediately recognize that something is wrong (in this case, the message "lunch starts at one thirty" was typed with the typists fingers starting on the wrong row of a typewriter). Mistypings and grammatically incorrect instructions are equally troublesome to computers, and the machines normally respond to such gibberish with reports, such as "incorrect or unintelligible command."

Unfortunately, some typographical errors are much more difficult to spot, even when programs are subject to extensive review and proofreading. As a simple example, consider the following statement that might be used in a program to define the mathematical constant π to 30 decimal places.

```
Const pi = 3.141592653589793234862643383279
```

In this statement, it turns out that the eighteenth and nineteenth decimal digits (the 4 and 8) are reversed, but that fact will be missed in most proofreading. The number seems to start correctly $3.14159\ldots$, and only a very careful reading and check with a reference source will allow this difficulty to be found. Typographical errors in constants can lead to systematic errors in computations throughout programs, but such difficulties can be extremely hard to find.

Similar trouble may arise when a statement looks reasonable, but contains a subtle error. Again, as an analogy, you might consider if you have ever been given directions to someone's house when a mistake was made (perhaps you were told to turn right instead of left or perhaps the desired road was at the fourth traffic light instead of the third you were told). When such an error is buried in the middle of a full page of instructions, it can be very hard to determine what happened, even when you discover the error.

In a programming environment, it is not uncommon for subtle, typographical errors to escape detection when programs are subjected to extensive review and testing. Code may even work in many cases, and failure may be noted only when an unusual situation arises.

Example: Mariner 1[7] – The July 22, 1962 launch of the Mariner 1 space probe to Venus gives a particularly good illustration of how a seemingly trivial typographical error can have dramatic consequences in computer programs. The program controlling that rocket should have contained the line

```
Do 3 I = 1, 3
```

instructing the computer to repeat a particular series of instructions several times. Instead, the comma was replaced by a period:

```
Do 3 I = 1.3
```

which assigned the value 1.3 to a variable called *Do3I*. As a result, the probe veered off course shortly after launch and had to be destroyed by mission control officers. Here a simple typographical error caused the loss of an $18.5 million probe and launch vehicle. Unfortunately, when programs are tens of thousands of lines long, finding a mistake in a single character is extremely difficult, if not impossible.

Distributed Computing. While typographical errors are conceptually simple errors (even if they may be hard to find), errors involving computer networks can be extremely sophisticated and subtle. Typically, a computer network involves several computers connected, so that various machines can gain access to data scattered throughout the network and so that the data needed for processing in one computer may be supplied by processing requests given to other machines. Two examples can illustrate some extremes for computer networks. A relatively simple network might consist of two or three computers in the offices of an insurance agency. Here, each agent and each secretary might have their own machine on their desk for their convenience, but all machines might be connected to some central files containing rate information. In addition, drafts of letters might be typed by secretaries at one computer, then reviewed by an agent at another computer, and finally printed by an assistant at a third machine. Here, each computer might be reasonably self-contained for word processing, but various machines need access to the same documents and insurance rate information.

A much more complex network connects banks around the country to the federal banking system and to various automatic teller machines (ATMs) located around the country. In this context, each bank may maintain its own computers to process its own accounts and records. When a customer at one bank, however, wants to cash a check from another bank, or when a customer uses an ATM located in another city, then the computers must communicate with each other. For either the cashing of a check or a ATM transaction, processing may start at one site, but a local computer must gain balance information from a distant machine in order to complete the translation. Thus, one computer must request information from another, the second computer must process the request, the second computer then responds to the first one, and the initial computer finally can finish handling the customer's request. (When banks are distant, it is possible that such requests might be relayed from one machine to another in a long chain until the initial query can be processed and an answer returned.)

In such a networking environment, processing must proceed at two levels. First, each individual computer will have transactions to process and local tasks to perform. Second, computers must interact with other machines. In considering this situation, the work at the local level generally may be viewed as being analogous to the work done in any computer. Issues of specifications, algorithms, coding, and errors all arise, but these are all constrained within separate machines. In large measure, then, transactions within an individual computer within a network may be viewed as being quite similar to tasks done in isolated machines. Putting computers in a network may not have much impact on this aspect of processing.

Interactions between machines, however, greatly expand the possibilities for error and raise the complexity of processing considerably. Many of these difficulties arise when different machines try to work with the same data or when separate machines must synchronize their processing. Difficulties with accessing common data are illustrated in the following simple example.

Example: A Bank Account Transfer – In processing a withdrawal of $50 from a checking account (initial balance $600) through an ATM, a computer might use these steps.

1. Determine old balance ($600) in the account.
2. Deduct the $50 withdrawal.
3. Record the new balance ($550) in the account.

This outline works quite well until both a husband and wife are on business in separate cities and each decide to withdrawal $50 from different ATM machines at the same time. If these transactions are processed in parallel, the following steps might occur concurrently.

Processing Husband's Request	Processing Wife's Request
1. Determine old balance ($600).	1. Determine old balance ($600).
2. Deduct the $50 withdrawal.	2. Deduct the $50 withdrawal.
3. Record the new balance ($550).	3. Record the new balance ($550).

In this case, since the two requests were processed at the same time, work on each request started with the same balance ($600), and the final balance given for each request was the same ($550). Thus, each person received $50 for a total of $100, but only $50 was deducted from the account.

This simple example is typical of the troubles that can arise when multiple transactions are to be processed at the same time. For each transaction, work may be straightforward, but complications can arise when several tasks occur simultaneously. In this case, there is no way to anticipate which spouse will make the request first or which ATM s will be used. Thus, the banks (and their programmers) cannot anticipate what sequence will be followed in the processing, and it may happen that different sequences could be followed on different days. In such cases, it may be necessary to place constraints upon when and how data are accessed and what processing is done when and where. Such possibilities can greatly complicate what might otherwise seem to be a reasonably straightforward task.

Similar issues can arise when a single computer is used to handle requests from several terminals at once, and algorithms have been developed and studied to handle many of these difficulties reasonably well. Additional research applies to processing involving many computers, although here there are more issues. Different computers may work differently, they may run at different speeds, and they may have different capabilities. Each of these factors greatly complicates analysis, and it is often difficult to anticipate how various interactions may affect possible results. In practice, coordination issues arise in computer networks with annoying frequency.

Another type of synchronization problem may arise in computer networks when several machines must work together to produce a final result. Some of the complexity of this aspect of computer networks is illustrated by communications for the first space shuttle orbital flight.

Example: Space Shuttle[8] – Computers on the first space shuttle orbital flight included five machines. For reliability, four machines were identical, and they were connected in a way to allow results from each to check each other. Further, in case one failed completely and then another, the system could still be brought back to full capability with the remaining two. After some initial work with these four machines, a fifth machine of a different type was added to increase reliability further. This fifth computer was to monitor the data input to the other four and to review selected results. In case of a failure, astronauts were able to switch quickly from one system to another.

Operation of this computer network required the various computers to be synchronized; data from sensors and the crew had to be communicated to all machines at the same time. This requirement for synchronization was built into the specifications and algorithms for the first four machines, although some changes were needed when the fifth computer was added.

On the morning of April 10, 1981, before the launch was attempted, synchronization was lost for some processes, and that difficulty expanded later on the day of the launch. As a result, the launch was cancelled for that day; it took place two days later without further software problems.

In reviewing the causes for this synchronization problem, it seems that various tasks, when working in isolation, were performing appropriately. It was only the interaction of a combination of tasks that prevented the group of four computers from linking correctly with the fifth.

This difficulty of requiring appropriate communications among computers also brings up three other points. First, it seems that the timing problems that led to the synchronization failure came about because of various changes to the original requirements, algorithms, and coding. To begin with, the addition of the fifth machine to the network caused a fundamental change in the requirements. Now computers had to interact with a new computer of a different type than was anticipated originally. This change in requirements caused a variety of changes in algorithms; data were recorded in the system following a somewhat different pattern than originally anticipated. This design change allowed another error to disrupt communications during the first launch attempt.

Beyond the design changes involved in adding the fifth computer, other modifications were made in how the computers were started or initialized. In effect, a change made about two years before the launch caused the timing on the first four computers to be delayed briefly, relative to the fifth computer. The four computers all viewed this delay from the same perspective, so it had no effect on communications among themselves. However, the fifth computer viewed timing differently, and it was this fifth computer that could not be synchronized with the others.

Second, Murphy's Law does apply to software in real settings. In this case, analysis has since indicated that the synchronization problems for this launch might arise with only a 1 in 67 probability. The chances for failure were quite low, and no problems were encountered either during earlier tests or during the launch two days later. However, during the first actual launch, this low-probability problem struck. There was a potential for something to go wrong, and it did.

Third, while the shuttle Orbiter was protected against hardware failure by the replication of elements (such as sensors and computers), this addition of elements added greatly to the complexity of the software. In this duplicated environment, the mission could proceed even when individual components failed. Additional complexity, however, also greatly increased the chances of logical errors in computer programs, and interrelationships between parts of the computer programs were much more difficult to identify, test, and validate. In the end, some of these interrelationships worked together to cause the synchronization problems that led to the delay of the launch.

═══ TESTING ═══

Once programs are written, they may be tested in several ways. First, they may be run with special data where results are known. Then their output may be compared with the known, correct results. Initially this testing may focus on individual parts of a large program, but eventually tests should determine how well various parts function together. Second, programs may be tested by running them in a simulated environment. This may allow programs to operate under a variety of conditions that one might anticipate in actual operation. (More discussion of simulations is found in Chapter 7.) Third, programs may be run in an actual working environment, perhaps with backup procedures based on another system. In this work, errors can be noted.

Each of these types of tests exercises various parts of a program, and each can help developers find errors. It should be noted, however, that the goals of the people performing the testing can have a significant effect on the results. Specifically, if testers are actively trying to find errors, then they will design tests to cover a wide range of cases and conditions, covering unusual possibilities as well as the most common ones. On the other hand, if a group wants to show that code has few errors, then it may place less emphasis on cases that may be viewed as being risky.

In the best of all worlds, it might be desirable to test a program completely with all possible cases. In practice, however, such testing is almost never possible for the combinatorial explosion mentioned for algorithms in Chapter 4 interferes with testing as well. Usually there are simply too many cases and alternatives for testing to cover even a small fraction of the actual possibilities. As a result, software of any complexity simply cannot be tested completely, and the running of software in normal use will almost certainly cover cases that have not been tested. As a specific illustration, this difficulty is documented in the following statistics involving the space shuttle.

Example: Space Shuttle[9] – "The Space Shuttle Ground Processing System, with over 1/2 million lines of code, is one of the largest real-time systems ever developed. The stable release version underwent 2177 hours of simulation testing and ... 280 hours of actual use during the third shuttle mission." Errors detected during both testing and the actual mission were classified as "critical," "major," or "minor," and the occurrences of these errors is shown below.

	Critical	Major	Minor
Testing	3	76	128
Mission	1	3	20

Thus, while many errors were caught during extensive testing and simulation, a fair number of problems were not encountered until the mission itself.

═══ MAINTENANCE ═══

This chapter has already noted that one cause of the shuttle Orbiter launch delay involved changes that were made in the initial specifications. An additional machine was added to the Orbiter's computer network to provide further backup capabilities if errors occurred in one system.

More generally, maintenance of a software package always involves either corrections of previously identified errors or changes in specifications or algorithms to make the programs better or more useful. The goal of maintenance is to enhance the capabilities, correctness, or performance of a program. While these goals may be worthwhile, changes in software also provide an opportunity for new errors to be introduced into the system as well. As with the shuttle Orbiter launch delay, sometimes these errors can be particularly visible or disturbing. Two additional examples illustrate some of the range of difficulties that can arise.

Example: CTSS[10] – In the early 1960s, MIT's CTSS computer once printed out the file of passwords instead of the message of the day when people logged in. Here, the problem originated with one set of assumptions that were made when the system was first designed, but then forgotten later when the system was "improved." In this case, each user on the system was assigned one directory, with the assumption that the user would only be on one terminal at a time. In addition, when a user wanted to edit a file of data, a special temporary file was used for intermediate work and that file was given a particular name within the directory. All of this is reasonable when any user has only one terminal and will be editing one piece of work at a time. This policy, however, also applied to the system account, which is used to administer accounts and to manage various work on the computer as a whole. Later, when the system expanded, this assumption was forgotten, and several system administrators were allowed to log in at one time. As a result, when two administrators were editing at the same time, the computer confused which temporary files were which, and data involving passwords were exchanged with less sensitive information that was generally available.

Example: AT&T[11] – On January 15, 1990, long distance service of AT&T was disrupted for about nine hours due to a software error in the electronic switching systems (ESSs) used in the system. As with the MIT CTSS system, earlier versions of the software to control ESSs worked correctly. This software was improved, however, to allow the network to respond more quickly when a switch malfunctioned, corrected the problem (often automatically), and came back into service. Unfortunately, a subtle error in this software meant that the recovery of one ESS could interfere with the functioning of those to which it was connected. (When a nearby switch determined that an ESS was working again, the communications between the machines "confused" the nearby switch, due to the programming error.) Since this same type of switch with the same software was used through the AT&T network, the disruption of one switch caused the failure of its neighbors, which in turn caused the failure of more neighbors, and so forth through the national telephone network. Thus, one problem spread from ESS to ESS through the system until the entire network experienced difficulty.

This ESS example again illustrates several points that are common to many software failures. First, the new ESS software had been tested extensively before it was released for general use, and even then it worked nicely for about a month without particular problems. Second, in addition to testing, it is standard procedure to conduct reviews of code during development. Thus, the code containing the error was subject to reviews by teams of programmers; the error was made by one programmer, but many others would have had the chance to correct it. Third, the shutdown of the system was triggered by a relatively uncommon sequence of events, and it would be quite difficult to anticipate this sequence. Fourth, since the previous code worked correctly, it was the desire to improve the code during maintenance that introduced a new error into previously correct programs.

Finally, these difficulties with the ESS software highlight a more general principle that has evolved with regard to the maintenance of large software packages. Specifically, E. N. Adams[12] has estimated that 15% to 50% of the attempts to remove an error from a large program result in the introduction of one or more additional errors. (The frequency may vary from package to package, but the likelihood of introducing new errors is nontrivial in any case.) Thus, experience with large control programs (with between 100,000 and 2,000,000 lines of code) leads Adams to conclude[13] that only a small fraction of known errors should be corrected.

═══ VERIFICATION ═══

With the great potential described in this chapter for making errors in programs, it is important to note that much effort has gone into the development of problem-solving techniques, the writing of specifications and algorithms, the production of programs, and the testing of systems. Formal approaches have evolved that can be of significant value in reducing the number of errors in code, and such work is often (but not always) used in the development of code today. For example, each system mentioned in this chapter used rigorous development methods, and these methods certainly helped developers to detect and correct errors. The discussion in this chapter, however, also indicated that even these formal methods were not enough to avoid all significant errors.

In reviewing many of these formal methods, it should be noted that each approach normally focuses on one aspect of the development process, often the writing of specifications or the design of algorithms. No formalism can anticipate all of what is intended in the specification of a problem, but some methods can help find omissions and inconsistencies. Such approaches also can help developers identify assumptions behind various pieces of code, so that the maintenance of programs will be less likely to contradict previous assumptions. Without a crystal ball, however, no system can anticipate what might have been meant when plans for a system were first made, and there is little hope that any formal system could solve all of the difficulties related to specifications.

In the development of code from specifications, however, formal proof methods have been developed that enable certain types of programs to be proved correct in a mathematical sense. In these methods, initial conditions and final desired results are stated in terms of formal logic, and logical (or mathematical) proofs are developed to show a code segment will work in all possible cases. Following these techniques, some moderate-sized programs have been proven to meet their specifications, and some chips have also been demonstrated to be correct. In each case, the work has shown that the programs or hardware will work in all possible circumstances, according to the specifications given. In the long term, such methods permit one to hope that future large programs can be written to their specifications without errors. If programs can be shown to be logically correct following their specifications, then many current troubles with software would be eliminated. Issues already described regarding the writing of specifications would still be troublesome, but the writing of code from specifications would not introduce more errors. This suggests that formal program verification has the potential to improve the quality of software packages significantly.

Currently, formal verifications are used with some frequency for verifying the correctness of computer chips, and some of this work has been particularly impressive. For example, in 1990 the Programming Research Group of Oxford University, headed by C. A. R. Hoare, together with IN-MOS Ltd., received the Queen's Award for Technological Achievement for the development of a chip to perform arithmetic with real numbers. Formal methods were used to prove that the chip met all of its specifications. Further, work was done in parallel by this theoretically oriented group and a more traditional testing group. According to one news report,[14]

> The race [between the two groups] was won by the formal development method—it was completed an estimated 12 months ahead of what otherwise would have been achievable. Moreover, the formal design pointed to a number of errors in the informal one that had not shown up in months of testing. The final design was of higher quality, cheaper, and was completed quicker.

Such successes suggest that formal verification techniques may eventually allow the error-free development of complex software systems. In the short term, however, the value of this formal approach is the subject of considerable debate, for several reasons. First, the complexity of chips often is considerably lower than that of software. Successes at the hardware level should be expected first, since the problems at that level are often more manageable. Second, formal specifications can be extremely difficult to write for some types of processing. For example, it is difficult to write formal specifications that capture the problems of numerical error mentioned earlier in this chapter. Third, formal methods have never been successfully applied to very large programs, and it may not be clear that techniques that work for a few thousand lines of code can be scaled up to handle programs that are tens or hundreds of thousands of lines long. Fourth, since formal methods involve logical proofs of statements (as in mathematics), there can always be the question of whether proofs constructed by humans are correct. A single incorrect deduction can render a proof incorrect, and some argue that the chances are very good that an error will be made in thousands of lines of a proof. It is not impossible that some aspects of a proof could be automated, but then the validity of the proof would involve the correctness of the proof-checking program. Overall, it can be said that considerable progress is being made in this area of program verification, but the application of these techniques to very large programs still may be years away.

═══ COST OF CORRECTNESS ═══

Many of the issues raised in this chapter depend upon the size and complexity of the problem under consideration. In general, simple problems often have short, simple solutions. Such programs can be reviewed extensively, and formal verification techniques can be applied without great difficulty to prove that the solutions are correct. For example, programs for easy problems in a first semester programming class may involve 100 or 200 lines of code, and certainly professionals can manage such programs easily.

Unfortunately, however, few real programs consist of only a few hundred lines of code. For example, a word processor for a personal computer may involve 10,000 to 50,000 lines of code. A similar amount of code is required for the UNIX[15] operating system, which performs many of the administrative and managerial functions required on many computers. The in-flight control systems for the space shuttle is reported as requiring about 500,000 lines, and projections for the size of the software for the Strategic Defense Initiative (SDI or "Star Wars") range between 10 million and 100 million lines.

With these real programs, error rates for the software industry typically average between eight and ten errors per thousand lines of code, although significantly lower rates have been achieved. For example, in 1989 the on-board software for the space shuttle achieved what was called an "exemplary" error rate of only 0.1 errors per thousand lines.[16] Even with that rate, however, the program of 500,000 lines of code would still contain about 50 errors, and this chapter has previously described that one of the earlier errors in that code in 1981 caused the first shuttle orbital flight to be delayed. Further, this "exemplary" code was achieved at a cost of $1,000 per line, and the overall package cost NASA $500,000,000. (This code also highlights the difficulties that can arise during the maintenance of code as reports indicate some 4,000 changes being made in this shuttle software between 1981 and 1985. This would translate to roughly 1,000 per year or perhaps three per day, including holidays and weekends!) Projects like the shuttle do suggest that techniques are currently available to produce significantly better programs, but 50 errors in a program can hardly be classified as "error-free."

As computers are used to tackle more and more complex problems, programs become longer and more sophisticated, and it becomes virtually impossible to be assured that they will work perfectly in actual situations. This message is reinforced by an article[17] by John Garman, former Deputy Chief of the NASA's Spacecraft Software Division, reporting on the delayed first launch of the shuttle orbital.

> The development of avionics software for the Space Shuttle is one of the largest, if not <u>the</u> largest, flight software implementation efforts ever undertaken in this nation. It has been very expensive, and yet it has saved money, saved schedule, and increased design margins time and time again during the evolution of the Orbiter and its ground test, flight tests, and finally the STS-1 mission. Since computers are programmed by humans, and since "the bug" was in a program, it must surely follow that the fault lies with some human programmer or designer somewhere – maybe! But I think that's a naive and shortsighted view, certainly held by very few within the project. It is complexity of design and process that got us (and Murphy's Law!). Complexity in the sense that we, the "software industry"[,] are still naive and forge into large systems such as this with too little computer, budget, schedule, and definition of the software role. We do it because these systems won't work, can't work, without computers and software.

══ SUMMARY ══

1. Program correctness can be measured in several ways: program verification refers to how well a program meets its specification, while validation refers to how well a program solves the actual problem that people are trying to solve.

2. Errors can arise for many reasons: specifications can have omissions and inconsistencies, algorithms may be incorrect, numeric computations may be the subject of roundoff or numerical errors, and typographical errors may occur. In addition, new errors may be introduced to previously correct code when changes or corrections are made during maintenance. Distributing computing, with many computers joined on a single network, can compound the complexity of code and introduce new types of errors.

3. For large programs, experience shows that errors will always be present. Average error rates in the computer industry may be as high as 8 to 10

errors per 1,000 lines, although the software for the space shuttle was significantly better at 0.1 errors per 1,000 lines. Even when few errors are present, however, the software for the first shuttle flight demonstrates that a single error may be enough to prevent the code from working correctly when it is needed.

4. When errors are found in large programs, experience demonstrates that the correction of one error is reasonably likely to introduce one or more new errors. Thus, it is usually unwise even to try to correct all known errors in large programs.

5. Formal program verification techniques may be a promising way to reduce the error rate for software or perhaps even to eliminate errors completely, although such an approach has not been applied as yet to very large programs. Even if programs are correct according to their specifications, however, difficulties with writing specifications may still mean that programs do not solve actual problems as desired.

═══ CONCLUSIONS AND IMPLICATIONS ═══

At the present time, all large programs contain errors, and the same situation can be expected for the foreseeable future. Techniques are known to improve program correctness and reliability, but experience and practice demonstrate that errors will always be present in code. It is possible that processing will proceed as desired in any particular run of a program, but in practice Murphy was right, "Anything that can go wrong, will." Thus, policy that depends upon software must anticipate that errors will occur, and the very nature of these errors suggests that one cannot anticipate how or when they will happen. Policies simply cannot assume that software will work correctly.

In the context of the Strategic Defense Initiative (SDI), this was stated eloquently in an open letter by Gary Chapman, Executive Director of the Computer Professionals for Social Responsibility, to the members of the United States Congress:

> Today, all computer scientists agree that the software developed for any strategic defense will have errors or "bugs." . . .
>
> Department of Defense officials and some computer scientists have defended the SDI by saying that although the software may have "bugs," these errors will not make a significant difference in the performance

of the system, or that they will degrade the system only partially, leaving enough resources to complete the mission of space-based missile defense.

This argument is groundless. The effects of unknown errors in software are clearly impossible to predict or anticipate. A single error in the SDI's software could cause complete system failure under unpredictable conditions. The mathematical character of computer systems is such that tiny errors can have major effects. ... While one Pentagon consultant has claimed that the SDI could have "100,000 errors and still function," Professor David Parnas, one of the world's leaders in software engineering, has said, "This is true, but only if you pick your errors very carefully." Obviously this is impossible.

A similar argument applies to virtually any complex computer system, and planning must always consider what actions will be necessary in handling a problem when (not if) computer programs fail.

≡ DISCUSSION QUESTIONS ≡

6.1 Chapter 3 stated the Halting Problem and proved that this problem was not solvable. It is impossible to develop an algorithm that will determine if any specified program will halt with any specified input. (Of course, it may be easy to determine if some programs will halt, but Chapter 3 demonstrated that no algorithm is possible for handling all programs with all inputs.)

One part of program correctness normally involves whether a program will halt (or will produce an appropriate answer in a finite amount of time). Discuss how the unsolvability of the Halting Problem implies that no algorithm is possible to determine if any programs will meet its specifications for all inputs. Thus, programs will never be able to formally verify the correctness of all software, given only the specifications.

6.2 In considering the task of automating program testing, do you think it would be easier to write a correct program or to write a program that correctly checks whether another program is correct?

Would your answer be affected by whether the problem was given using formal specifications?

Would your answer be affected by whether a series of known test cases had been developed?

6.3 Who do you think should be considered ethically or legally liable when incorrect programs cause injury or damage?

NOTES

1 Traditionally, mistakes and oversights in computer programs have been called **bugs**. Edsger Dijkstra, a world-renowed computer scientist, has suggested that such terminology can foster the image that errors are beyond a programmer's control — a bug might creep into a program when no one is looking. At the very least, he argues, such terminology seems to suggest that a certain number of bugs are normal and should be expected; some "reasonable" number of bugs may be acceptable in programs.

In contrast, he argues that errors in programs should be labeled directly as errors, and such mistakes should not be tolerated in programs any more than in the construction of buildings or bridges. Following this suggestion, this chapter consistently uses the words *error* or *mistake* instead of bug when referring to the inappropriate functioning of a computer program. See Edsger Dijkstra, "On the Cruelty of Really Teaching Computing Science," *Communications of the ACM*, Volume 32, Number 12, December 1989, p. 1402.

2 In elementary school, the author once got the correct answer to a long division problem, although the work contained two errors. The author first multiplied incorrectly, and this was followed by an incorrect subtraction. In this case, the two mistakes "cancelled out," and the final result showed no error at all. This was one case where two wrongs did make a right.

3 For more information, see William Broad, "Computers and the U.S. Military Don't Mix," *Science*, Volume 207, March 14, 1980, p. 1183, and quoted in *Software Engineering Notes*, Volume 11, Number 5, October 1986, p. 17.

4 For more information, see Nathaniel Borenstein, "My Life as a NATO Collaborator," *Bulletin of the Atomic Scientists*, April 1989, pp. 14–20.

5 Here one might argue that these numbers should be rounded to seven digits rather than just ignoring the eighth digit. In that case, the first number would round to 12,345,680, and the difference would be 10, which is much closer. This approach can work well for some numbers, but errors can still be large. In this rounding case, for example, consider $123,456,751 - 123,456,749$ where the answer should be 2. Rounding to seven places, however, gives $123,456,800 - 123,456,700$ and the difference reported is 100. Thus, rounding numbers is not much more helpful in accounting for errors than simply ignoring the last digit(s).

6 Reported in *Software Engineering Notes*, Volume 11, Number 5, October 1986, p. 9.

7 *Annals of the History of Computing,* 1984, Volume 6, Number 1, p. 6, reported in *Software Engineering Notes*, Volume 8, Number 5, October 1983, p. 4, with

further editorial comment in Volume 11, Number 5, October 1985, p. 17.

8   For a reasonably detailed account of what happened prior to the launch of the first space shuttle, see John R. Garman, "The "Bug" Heard 'Round the World," *Software Engineering News*, Volume 6, Number 5, October 1981, pp. 3–10. Mr. Garman was the Deputy Chief of the Spacecraft Software Division of the NASA Johnson Space Center.

9   Misra, "Software Reliability Analysis," *IBM System Journal*, Volume 22, Number 3, 1983. Quoted in *Software Engineering Notes*, Volume 11, Number 5, October 1989, p. 16.

10   Reported by Bob Morris and Ken Thompson, with additional notes from Fernando J. Corbato, in *Software Engineering Notes*, Volume 15, Number 2, April 1990, pp. 18–19.

11   More information may be found in many accounts. See, for example, "Can We Trust Our Software?" *Newsweek*, January 29, 1990, pp. 70–73. A more technical treatment may be found in *Software Engineering Notes*, Volume 15, Number 2, April 1990, pp. 11–14.

12   E. N. Adams, "Optimizing Preventing Service of Software Products," *IBM Journal of Research and Development,* Volume 28, Number 1, January 1984, p. 8

13   *op. cit.,* p. 12.

14   David Gries, "Queen's Awards Go to Oxford University Computing and IN-MOS," *Computing Research News*, Volume 2, Number 3, July 1990, p. 11.

15   UNIX is a registered trademark of AT&T.

16   Edward J. Joyce, "Is Error-Free Software Achievable?" *Datamation*, February 15, 1989, pp. 53, 56.

17   John Garman, *op. cit.*, p. 9.

simulation

1a. The action or practice of simulating, with intent to deceive; false pretence, deceitful profession

 b. Tendency to assume a form resembling that of something else; unconscious imitation

2. A false assumption or display, a surface resemblance or imitation, *of* something

3. The technique of imitating the behavior of some situation or process (whether economic, military, mechanical, etc.) by means of a suitably analogous situation or apparatus, esp. for the purpose of study or personnel training

—From *The Oxford English Dictionary, Second Edition,* Oxford University Press, New York, and Clarendon Press, 1989, by permission of Oxford University Press.

Simulation

S imulation is an exciting area of research today. The last alternative of the dictionary definition just given suggests that simulations may use apparatus (e.g., computing equipment) to imitate behavior, make predictions, study the effects of actions based upon underlying theories, or help train people. With the widespread availability of computers, machines simulate many situations where physical experiments would take too long or be too dangerous. For example, computers simulate dangerous conditions in nuclear reactors or during the flight of aircraft to help in the training of reactor operators and pilots. Expanding this role of simulation, the U. S. Government is developing a multibillion dollar computing facility, called the National Test Bed, to allow testing of simulation models on a massive scale, perhaps permitting large-scale studies of conditions of nuclear war.

This chapter studies this common use of computers in some detail; as with earlier chapters, the conclusions about simulation are mixed. There is no doubt that simulation can help provide important insights and help solve problems. The dictionary definitions of the word *simulation*, however, also refer to "intent to deceive," "pretence," "false assumption or display," and "deceitful profession." Unfortunately, simulation in computing can also have these qualities.

═══ WHAT IS IT?/HOW DOES IT WORK? ═══

In computing, the technique of simulation depends upon capturing the important characteristics from a situation in a formal (often mathematical) model. Conclusions about the situation then are derived from the model, often using computers to perform computations. The following example illustrates and clarifies this basic notion of modeling.

Example: Family Size Simulation. Consider the following problem:

> A young couple decides to have children until they have at least one boy and one girl, and then they plan to stop having children. How many children might they expect to have overall?

This problem is typical of many that try to anticipate the future. First, the couple cannot know exactly how large their family will become until they have enough children to include one boy and one girl. Second, some general bounds may seem reasonable. The couple certainly will have at least two children, and one might expect that at least one boy and one girl would have arrived by the time they had ten children. (On the other hand, one sometimes hears stories about a couples that have raised ten or fifteen children, all of whom were girls.) Third, while exact outcomes cannot be determined ahead of time, one could investigate birth records of many families. Parameters or guidelines for such research, however, might be difficult to determine. For example, as a first step, one might consider families that had both boys and girls to see how many children were born before both boys and girls were included. But with this approach, one might wonder if the selection of families with both boys and girls biased the results; conclusions might be different if large families of all boys or all girls were included.

Two other approaches to this problem might try to reformulate it in scientific and mathematical terms and then use techniques of science and mathematics to gain insights into appropriate results. For example, one might use probability and algebra to reduce this problem to a series of formulae and equations which could then be solved by mathematics. Alternately, the formulation of the problem using probability and algebra might allow one to conduct an experiment to gain insight into the desired conclusions.

To be more specific, consider the following approach. To begin, one might make the following assumptions:

1. The probability of a baby being a boy might be assumed to be the same as the probability of a baby being a girl. (Actually probabilities are slightly higher for girls than for boys, but one might choose to ignore small differences in favor of simplicity in the model.)

2. The gender of one baby might be assumed to be independent of the genders of all previous babies. (This assumption would imply that a girl and a boy were both equally likely, even if a couple previously had eight consecutive boys or eight consecutive girls.)

With these two assumptions, it would seem that the gender of successive babies was as random as the outcome of heads or tails in flipping a fair coin. In each case, there are two equally likely outcomes (girl/boy or head/tail), and successive results do not depend upon previous history. With this analogy, it would seem that one could gain insights into the number of children for the couple mentioned by counting the number of times a coin is flipped until both a head and a tail are obtained. (Certainly flipping a coin is much faster and less expensive than having children, so this might seem to be a cost effective way of studying the problem at hand.) The following table shows the results for ten different experiments, conducted as this material was written. Here, H stands for a head and T stands for a tail.

		Number	Number	Total
Experiment	Sequence	Heads	Tails	Flips
1	T, T, H	1	2	3
2	H, H, T	2	1	3
3	H, H, H, T	3	1	4
4	T, H	1	1	2
5	H, T	1	1	2
6	H, H, H, T	3	1	4
7	T, H	1	1	2
8	T, T, T, T, T, H	1	5	6
9	H, H, T	2	1	3
10	T, T, H	1	2	3

In this particular test, coins were flipped until at least one head and one tail was obtained. The results show that a total of 32 coin flips were required for the ten experiments, so an average of 3.2 coins were flipped per experiment. The lowest number of flips was 2, and that number occurred three times, while the highest number was 6 and that occurred only once. One might also note that altogether both 16 heads and 16 tails were obtained. Since these numbers are equal, it seems reasonable to conclude that on any given toss obtaining a head or a tail was equally likely and the process of tossing the coin was fair.

Returning to the question of family size, this table does not say anything directly about how many children the couple might expect to have. The remarks, however, do suggest that the results for flipping coins until a head and a tail occurred might be quite similar to the experiences of couples wanting both a boy and a girl. If those remarks are correct, therefore, the experiment in the table might suggest that the couple would expect to have about three children and the most likely range would be two to four children. Experiment 8 cautions, however, that the couple should be prepared for a family size of six, since that did occur in one of the ten (10%) of the experiments.

Before concluding this family size example, it is worthwhile to consider how more data might be collected. If experiments are to continue, one approach would be to continue flipping coins. Such an approach, however, is time consuming; the coin tossing here took the author about ten minutes. For each experiment, coins had to be gathered and flipped one at a time, and the results had to be recorded. As an alternate approach, one might program a computer to pick successive heads and tails randomly and have the computer record the results. In this context, the use of the computer can allow a review of the number of heads and tails for thousands of experiments in a short amount of time.

The family size example illustrates many aspects of **simulation**, where important characteristics of a problem are identified and then used to determine likely outcomes or results. Simulations allow one to gain insights to a problem by studying a formal mathematical system or by conducting experiments. The next three sections look at this process of simulation in more detail.

Assumptions. The first task in a simulation is to identify important characteristics of the situation and to state properties in precise terms. In this process, a researcher determines what points seem significant, while extraneous details are omitted. For example, in the family size simulation, the statement was made that, "The probability of a baby being a boy might be assumed to be the same as the probability of a baby being a girl." Details of the hair color or age of the couple were ignored as were questions of where the couple lived and their socioeconomic circumstances. Similarly, it was assumed that the gender of one child was not related to the genders of any previous children and that the couple would not try to influence the gender of successive children in any way. Simulation, therefore, begins with a process of selection and with a series of assumptions about the problem under study. Altogether the collection of details and assumptions is called a **model** for the problem. A model is a precise statement of relevant characteristics and assumed properties for the problem under consideration.

Through this selection and hypothesis making, it is important to realize that different choices are possible. For the family size problem, a different model would result if the first assumption were changed so that 51% or 52% of all babies were girls. Similarly, the model might change if the couple paid attention to recent reports that relate the gender of a child to the time of conception within a woman's ovulation cycle. Changing any of these assumptions or adding any new factors to the study would alter the model for this problem, although the conclusions of a simulation might or might not change.

Modeling. The identification of assumptions and properties provides the starting point for modeling or simulation. Following this step, one works with the model to reach conclusions about the model, and these in turn are translated to give some results about the initial problem. Schematically, this process is shown in Figure 7-1.

In the overall process, the statement of assumptions and properties defines a specific model. The next step uses these statements to reach conclusions about the model. For example, the model for the family size simulation also applied to flipping coins, and several experiments were run to obtain results about the model. Finally, interpretations of these results suggested possible insights about the size of families, which formed the basis for the original problem.

In considering the middle step in the figure, it should be noted that work often may proceed in several ways to obtain results. In the family size

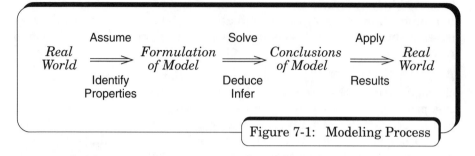

Figure 7-1: Modeling Process

simulation, experiments were run following the rules of the model. An alternate approach might translate the assumptions into appropriate equations. Thus, in determining family size, the definition of expected value in probability might lead to an equation, such as

$$E = \sum_{n=2}^{\infty} n \left(\frac{1}{2}\right)^{n-1} \quad .$$

Such equations then may be solved to give results.

This second step is also the part in the process that most often utilizes computers. For example, the computer may be used to automate experimentation, so that many trials can be done in a short period of time. Alternately, when many computations are required, the computer may perform the detailed steps efficiently. In this role, a model is already determined before computations begin, and the computer merely is instructed to follow steps prescribed in the model. When such steps require a large number of computations, the use of high-speed computers may make the difference between whether or not one can obtain results in a reasonable amount of time.

Conclusions. While the conclusions from a model always depend upon the particular assumptions and properties specified at the start, these results may be used in several ways. From a narrow perspective, a simulation may provide a simple answer to the original question. Thus, for the family size problem, the simulation indicated that the couple might expect to have 3.2 children before having exactly one boy and one girl.

From a broader perspective, however, a simulation may produce a range of conclusions that can be compared with previously known results or with the results of new experiments. A comparison of predictions of the model with real data then can help determine whether the original assumptions appear correct or whether refinements or corrections seem appropriate. For example, the family size simulation not only gives an average number of children but also some results on the number of times couples might have 2, 3, 4, or more children before having a child of each gender. This frequency data then might be compared with statistics available on the genders of the first 2, 3, 4 or more children in actual families. Similarities between the frequencies from the simulation and those from real data would tend to support the original assumptions, while large discrepancies might suggest that new or modified assumptions are needed. Then, when refinements are made in a model, new predictions can be obtained and checked again with the real world. In this broader context, simulation need not be the simple, linear path of Figure 7-1, where work starts with the formulation of a problem and concludes when the first results are obtained. Rather, the process of formulating properties, inferring results, and comparing with real data can be repeated several times to give better and better estimates. In this view, the process of modeling is closer to the directed triangle of Figure 7-2.

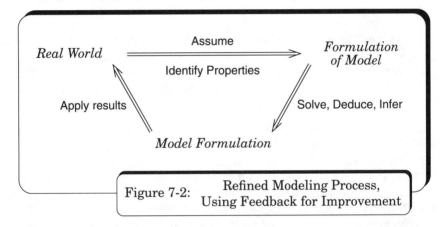

Figure 7-2:   Refined Modeling Process, Using Feedback for Improvement

With this broader view of modeling and simulation, finding results is only one part of a larger process of studying assumptions and selecting properties. When results are used to refine a model, hypotheses can be challenged, analyzed, and modified, and consequences of assumptions examined.

 **LIMITS**

Limitations of the approach of modeling may be identified by considering each of the basic steps shown in Figures 7-1 and 7-2. Since each part of a simulation builds upon the previous ones, any error or constraint at one point can affect all subsequent work, including any final conclusions.

Testing Assumptions. Both figures indicate that any simulation is built upon the assumptions and properties that are chosen at the very beginning. All subsequent work depends explicitly upon this first step, and any conclusions can only be as sound as the assumptions. While the importance of these assumptions may seem obvious, this observation has several practical consequences.

First, whenever possible, assumptions must be tested. Typically, this can be done in one of at least two ways.

1. Sometimes assumptions in a model are based upon a well developed scientific theory that has already been thoroughly studied. In a simulation of planetary motion, for example, work might be based upon Newtonian physics or upon the Theory of Relativity. Both of these topics are well understood. Constraints in Newtonian mechanics are widely known, and astronomers may be expected to agree upon what assumptions and properties are reasonable. In these circumstances, a large body of research may be used to validate statements in the initial formulation of the problem.

2. Sometimes the purpose of a simulation is to test assumptions; an initial model is constructed so that the consequences of properties can be examined. When predictions from a model agree with real data that can be examined, then the simulation process gives additional credibility to the initial assumptions.

In any testing, of course, one must be careful to avoid a chain of circular reasoning. If the purpose of a simulation is to test assumptions, then it is inappropriate to use those assumptions in evaluating the conclusions. For example, in logic, the implication $A \Rightarrow B$, or A *implies* B, is regarded as true whenever A is false, regardless of whether B is true or not. Similarly, the implication is true if B is true, regardless of whether A is true or not. Thus, the statement $A \Rightarrow B$ does not by itself say anything about the validity of either A or B. Rather the scientific method requires that predictions and theories always be evaluated against real experiments.

Second, if one has not proven that assumptions for a model are true and complete, then one must view any simulation results with some skepticism. For example, one should not fully trust the conclusions of the family size simulation, unless one can demonstrate that: (1) the two properties given are correct; and (2) there are no additional, independent properties that might affect the gender of successive children. If one does not believe that the assumptions about the gender of children in a family are the same as the assumptions about the occurrences of heads and tails in flipping a coin, then any action based upon the conclusions reached should be viewed as a bit of a gamble.

Third, when the assumptions of a model are not testable, then one cannot rely upon the answers. Moreover, questionable or invalid assumptions can undermine all further results; the further circumstances deviate from known, verified data, the less faith one should have in any results. When one cannot evaluate assumptions, conclusions must be regarded as speculation.

As an example, consider any simulation for missiles launched and exploding in a nuclear war. In this case, some information is currently known about behavior of missiles, about individual nuclear explosions, and about properties of radioactive materials. However, full-scale nuclear war extends substantially beyond any actual circumstances that have occurred, and assumptions for any simulation must be based on extrapolations of limited data. Until an actual war occurs, any assumptions cannot be compared with real data. For example, scientists discovered nuclear magnetic pulse (NMP) only after atomic bombs were used against Japan. The blasts produced effects that could not be explained by known principles, and a new property of atomic energy came to light. Therefore, in the context of modeling, any simulation of the dropping of these bombs prior to that time could not have included effects from NMP; the pulse simply was not known. Without a full-scale nuclear war, it is impossible to know whether other effects are still waiting to be discovered. The scale of such a cataclysmic event certainly is much greater than anything experienced to date, and there is no possible way to verify any set of assumptions for that context as being correct and complete. The conclusions of any such simulation, therefore, cannot be trusted and must be regarded as suspect.

This dependence of models on assumptions is particularly significant, because it is very tempting to use simulations when actual results are unknown. For example, one commonly hears about simulations to study effects from such factors as a reduction in the ozone layer or an increase in smog levels or elimination of large areas of the tropical rain forests. In each of these cases, the goal of a study is to look ahead at possible consequences of policies and then to select appropriate programs and principles to overcome undesired outcomes. Steps should be taken to avoid depletion of the ozone layer, if that will have catastrophic consequences for life on earth. However, it may be difficult to verify all assumptions in a model if predicted outcomes cannot be compared with real data. Some assumptions may follow from previous experiments and data, but one can still ask if a model includes all relevant properties.

Testing Programs. Once one formulates a model, the next step of a simulation involves solving equations, making deductions, and inferring results. When this step is done by computer, the question arises of how one knows if a computer program works correctly. As with the development of other types of programs, one could test various parts of a program and monitor the progress of a computation. In a traditional testing environment, however, a program is validated by running the program on data where results are known and then comparing expected results with those from the program.

When the goal of a simulation is to produce results for an unknown situation, however, testing becomes more difficult. In particular, when results for a data set are not known, then they cannot be used to check a program. This is a particular problem when a simulation (or other program) produces results that seem surprising. In this case, it may be difficult to determine if the unusual results are due to program errors or due to unexpected consequences of the model.

An example of this type of problem arose when satellites first analyzed the upper atmosphere, tabulated their findings, and reported the results to earth. In the analysis and tabulation stage, researchers had anticipated the possibility of experimental error from many sources, and computers on the satellites were programmed to make corrections for such errors, based on certain assumptions. Thus, satellites orbiting the Antarctic consistently corrected for an "obvious" experimental error showing a hole in the ozone layer. Readings were consistently modified during the data gathering and tabulation stages, and no hole was reported. Only after some months and after a review of some raw data did a scientist observe a consistent pattern indicating the presence of the hole in the ozone layer over the Antarctic. At this point, the correction procedures were turned off, and past raw data was re-evaluated showing a major, unexpected environmental phenomenon. Here the computer program on the satellite had been tested carefully on the basis of assumptions that had seemed reasonable, but no one had anticipated what the satellite would find. Thus, the valid conclusions were suppressed by the program, because they were considered obviously flawed. The same danger of unanticipated results can arise in simulations.

═══ ROLE AND USES ═══

Both the role and the value of simulations depend upon the fact that a simulation allows one to learn what conclusions follow from particular, specified assumptions and properties. This implies that simulations can be useful in either of two settings:

1. Simulations can help in identifying conclusions when models are based upon well established assumptions;

2. Simulations can provide insights about assumptions when conclusions can be compared with experimental data.

In practice, both approaches have been valuable in the study of various problems. Flight simulators, used in the training of airline pilots, illustrate the first of these uses. Such simulators are built upon assumptions and properties that have evolved over years of practical experience in flying airplanes. It is well documented how aircraft function under various conditions, and models can specify how aircraft will respond to various pilot actions.

This example also illustrates a particularly important application of simulations, where it is not practical to test conclusions under real conditions. For pilot training, it is very dangerous for them to fly actual aircraft when learning to respond to various conditions and emergencies. In an actual flight, incorrect judgment can result in aircraft collisions, with serious injuries, deaths, and costly damage. Such results clearly are unacceptable for training, and simulations based on known properties of flight can give pilots experience without risk of injury or damage.

The use of flight simulators also illustrates a potential difficulty with the use of simulation. In particular, even though assumptions in flight models can be verified, errors due to computer malfunctions or programming mistakes could be catastrophic. For example, pilots might learn from a simulation that one action was an appropriate response to a particular emergency. If the correctness of this action depended upon an error in a computer, however, then pilots might react in the same incorrect manner during an actual emergency.

Another type of use for simulation is illustrated when models are built to study the functioning of the economy. Part of a study may ask how factors, such as the money supply or the prime interest rate, affect the overall economy, as measured by the gross national product (GNP) or by the unemployment rate. While the exact connection between these factors may not be known, models can be developed that consider different relationships between economic factors. Once such models are constructed, they can be tested to determine if they predict changes in the economy already observed. When such predictions seem to agree with observations, insights may be given into relationships between variables in the model. Conversely, lack of agreement may suggest which relationships need re-examination.

In either of these cases, real data can be used to validate either the conclusions or the assumptions. The model then increases the understanding about the other parts of the model.

When neither the assumptions nor the conclusions can be effectively and completely tested, however, a simulation cannot produce strong evidence to support any position. Since the assumptions are not tested, the conclusions must be viewed as possibly invalid. Similarly, the assumptions must be viewed with skepticism, since the conclusions are untested.

Logically, this same limitation of simulations continues when several simulations with untestable conclusions and unverified assumptions all seem to agree. For example, such difficulties are highlighted when the Computer

Professionals for Social Responsibility (CPSR) argue against such defense programs as the Strategic Defense Initiative (SDI) or the "Brilliant Pebbles" program. In each case, hardware and software would be developed to defend against a ballistic missile attack, but CPSR argues, in part, that it is impossible to know beforehand all appropriate assumptions and properties concerning a full-scale nuclear attack. Thus, simulations cannot guarantee that systems work correctly.

Multiple simulations might show inconsistencies in logic if they produced different results. However, without thorough comparisons with real data, it is impossible to know if conclusions from one or many simulations are correct.

══ SUMMARY ══

1. A model is a precise statement of assumptions and properties that are meant to describe the important characteristics of a particular real situation. A simulation uses a model to determine logical consequences of the assumptions.

2. Simulations can be useful in two basic ways. First, when models are based upon established principles, then conclusions of a simulation can give important new insights. Second, assumptions in a model can be tested by comparing conclusions from a simulation with experimental data. Close agreement of predicted and actual data tends to support assumptions. Differences may suggest appropriate modifications for assumptions.

3. Any model must be tested against real data. While conclusions should always follow logically from assumptions, conclusions have little merit if the assumptions are false. Thus, in considering the results of a simulation, it is inadequate only to evaluate logical arguments within a model itself. Checks with the real world are essential. When one cannot verify experimentally that assumptions are true and complete, then one must view any results from a simulation with some skepticism.

4. Questions about the validity of a model are particularly important in those simulations that are designed to predict outcomes in circumstances that are too dangerous or too costly to allow the collection of real data. In these situations, it may be impossible to test conclusions experimentally from a model. This means that particular care is needed in verifying assumptions.

5. When computers are used to solve equations, make deductions, or infer results, then programs must be tested as well. Even when the assumptions of a model are correct, the conclusions can be wrong if a computer is not programmed correctly. This issue can be of particular significance in cases where results cannot be verified experimentally.

≡ CONCLUSIONS AND IMPLICATIONS ≡

Simulation can be quite appropriate when assumptions and/or conclusions are tested. However, conclusions from simulations with untested and untestable assumptions may be suspect. In such cases, one's response to those conclusions may depend upon an analysis of what may happen if the conclusions are correct and what outcomes could arise if the outcomes are incomplete or wrong. Two examples show the extremes that may arise in using simulations to influence policies.

1. In considering the ozone layer, many models and simulations indicate that depletion of the layer would be a significant threat to life. If the assumptions are correct, then only some unknown property or agent could prevent disaster without some action. In this case, policies must seek to prevent the depletion of this layer. Any other action would require a blind faith that the models were invalid, without any supporting evidence.

2. In considering a strategic defense program based on simulations of a massive launch of nuclear missiles, one might dream that countermeasures might work to prevent disaster if the models were correct. If the assumptions were wrong, however, then there would be no reason to believe the planned defense would be effective. In this case, disaster would result if one placed one's entire faith in the simulation, and prudence would require that alternate defense strategies also be implemented. (In this situation, since alternate approaches are needed in any case, one might question if the countermeasures based upon the untested models were cost effective.)

In each of these cases, any models may include many assumptions and properties that are well established, but these models also require one to go well beyond any known data. In each case, the models may give insights about what may happen, and steps might be taken to handle these anticipated situations. However, one must also consider what might happen if such models are wrong. In the case of the ozone layer, the possible outcomes from a correct model present a strong case for taking action to bolster the ozone layer. In the case of strategic defense, however, the value of a costly countermeasure must be evaluated with the knowledge that the models that form the basis for that counter-measure may be invalid.

═══ DISCUSSION QUESTIONS ═══

7.1 Investigate one application of simulation techniques (perhaps using the library as a resource). In your study, try to answer as many of the following questions as you can.

    a. What motivated the use of modeling rather than other techniques?

    b. What assumptions were used in the simulation?

    c. What algorithms or techniques were used in the simulation?

    d. What role did the computer play in the simulation?

    e. What conclusions were reached during the simulation process?

7.2 Find an article in the popular press concerning predictions about the earth's ozone layer. (Virtually all such predictions depend upon simulations, so try to find a statement that has involved some type of simulation.)

    a. Does the article indicate how these conclusions were obtained?

    b. Are the assumptions underlying these predictions identified?

    c. What conclusions can you draw about this particular simulation?

    d. Does your evaluation of this article lead you to any tentative conclusions about how results of simulations may be reported?

CHAPTER 8

To err is human –
To really foul things up takes a computer.

Human Factors

People are very creative and inventive in finding new and original ways to make mistakes. Early chapters of this book indicated that throughout the development of computer systems, human error can lead to a wide range of errors in the problem-solving process in general and in the production of software in particular. Many of the examples of system malfunctions can be attributed to people's mistakes or oversights. Unfortunately, people also demonstrate this same remarkable capacity for making mistakes in using and operating computer systems.

This natural capability for doing work incorrectly creates a conflicting tension for the development of computer systems. On the one hand, computer systems contain errors for many reasons, and this limits the level of trust that can be placed in computer systems. Such a conclusion suggests that people running computers must be given the capability to correct any system, so they can recover from mistakes as these errors are identified. On the other hand, people can make mistakes in running computers. The more that people are empowered to work freely with systems, the more likely they are to introduce new mistakes into data or processing. Such examples suggest that people running and using computers should be restricted in the operations they are allowed to perform.

This chapter considers a variety of ways in which people can make mistakes in running computers and then mentions some implications for the design and development of computer systems.

═══ DATA ENTRY ═══

Data entry errors comprise one of the simpliest yet most common forms of error. For example, most readers probably have encountered such errors occasionally in a store, when a clerk misreads a price or item number or presses the wrong buttons by mistake. Certainly in entering thousands of prices during a day, one can expect clerks to make mistakes, and customers are charged improper amounts on their bills.

To help counter such problems, additional checks or steps may be taken. For example, stock numbers may include check-digits, as described in Chapter 5. Alternatively, a cash register or computer may be programmed to check for certain types of errors. Thus, grocery items costing over $100.00 might be challenged. Such amounts might be possible when purchasing a side of beef, but such expenses are rare. Similarly, spelling checkers can monitor each word as it is entered and signal when an unknown word is encountered. In these cases, machines identify possible typographical errors as the information is typed, and people entering the data are given the chance to revise the information. In this approach to data entry errors, however, machines must allow unusual results to be typed. If unusual, but rare or unforeseen, values are prohibited, then users will find ways around a system, circumventing the checking process.

A cash register that prohibits the entry of items over $100.00 might encourage cashiers to enter several entries of $50.00 when the meat order for a picnic totals $150.00, for example. In this case, the cashier must enter a sequence of numbers totaling the desired charge, and the possibility of typographical errors for such a sequence may be relatively high. Further, the resulting bill will not directly show the single, high-cost item, so the bill will be relatively hard to check. As a second example, spelling checkers may have large dictionaries, but they cannot know all possible words that might arise such as proper names, technical terms, or words borrowed from foreign languages. When word processors prohibit the use of words not found in the dictionary, then either less appropriate terminology may be used or parts of a passage may be added manually, after the word processor has printed a draft document. In either case, the restrictions of the word processor would interfere with the production of the desired manuscript.

When the consequences of data entry errors are particularly severe, more drastic measures might be considered. For example, two different typists might enter the same information, the results of their work compared, and discrepancies resolved. To be more specific, back in the days when data were often stored on punch cards, utility companies sometimes duplicated typing in the preparation of electric or water bills as follows. One typist would enter data based on hand-written meter readings, producing a punched card. The same readings, together with the stack of cards, would then go to a second typist. This second typist would then place the cards in a special machine which would compare the holes in each card with what the second typist entered. When the two data sets were identical, the machine would cut a notch in the card in a special location, indicating the data had been verified. After working through a series of readings, therefore, the cards could be scanned visually to determine if all had the special notch. Cards without the notch could then be physically removed from the card deck and reviewed with the original data written by the meter reader. Today, such verification is still possible, although cards are often replaced by reels of tape or by disks, and the comparisons may be made electronically rather than by visual inspection.

Yet another approach to the problem involves automating the process, reducing the need for typists to enter data at all. Scanners in grocery stores, for example, read bar codes, so that product lists can be consulted and prices retrieved. With these scanners, clerks normally just move packages over laser sensors, eliminating manual data entry. Only special items (e.g., products not on file, fruit sold by weight) must be entered manually by a clerk. Similarly, in preparing utility bills, a meter reader may be given a portable computer that can be used to record his or her readings directly in machine-readable form, eliminating the need for a separate typing step.

While such automated systems certainly reduce the requirements of accuracy for a clerk, such scanners do not completely resolve all data entry problems. Instead correctness depends both upon the reliability of the scanners and upon the accuracy of the lists stored inside a machine. Here, however, the same issues arise. On the hardware side, a malfunctioning scanner may enter incorrect information, either sporadically or systematically. Thus, if the results from this automatic device are not reviewed carefully, mistakes could be found throughout a bill. (If you shop at a store that utilizes scanners, how carefully do you review the bill?)

At another level, with hundreds or thousands of stock numbers in a store, entering and updating inventory and price lists still requires hours of data entry. Clerks may no longer have to enter the price of every can of tomatoes, but some entry of prices still is required. And with hundreds of such prices, some data entry errors are still likely. Price lists may be reviewed carefully for accuracy, but in this context one error will affect the price of every item sold. Lists may be checked and rechecked, but any error will be compounded for each item sold.

Yet another type of problem involving scanners is illustrated in the following story.[1]

WATER SHUT-OFFS NOT INTENTIONAL

Pleasant Grove, Utah (AP). Pleasant Grove city officials say they have found and fixed the reason for several water users being cut off – despite having paid their bills. ... Pleasant Grove switched to a new envelope bill, replacing the postcard billing it had used for years. The new bills include an envelope for residents to mail their payments. ... however, ... the bar code printed on the envelope was for Orem rather than Pleasant Grove. As the bar codes are read electronically by automated postal equipment, when residents mailed their water payments, they went to Orem instead of Pleasant. ... the Pleasant Grove postmaster noticed the wrong bar code on some envelopes and asked postal employees to watch for the blue envelopes ... .

Automation and error checking can help identify errors. When errors occur, however, a single problem may affect many individual data items and many separate transactions.

≡ OPERATOR ERROR ≡

During the normal operation of most computing systems, processing often requires people to perform a variety of tasks. Various tasks may require data on specific tapes or disks, and these must be mounted on appropriate drives. Operations must be started, terminated, or monitored. New or modified hardware and software must be installed. Malfunctioning devices must be identified and removed from the system, and their work may need to be rerouted to alternate devices. All of this activity requires human interaction, and particularly large systems may demand enough attention to keep several people busy. On smaller systems, such demands are still present, but work may proceed on a smaller scale. (On personal computers, for example, most regular work may be limited to a simple moving of floppy disks in and out of a machine.)

Unfortunately, as with most human endeavors, any work done by a person operating a computer has the potential to be wrong. Computer operators can mount the wrong tape or put a correct tape onto the wrong drive. Similarly, operators may give a computer incorrect instructions. The following examples illustrate something of the range of opportunities for this type of error and some possible consequences.

- In a beginning programming class, a student working on a personal computer wanted to delete the files that contained the output from his program. The appropriate command was *del *.out*. Instead, the student forgot the suffix *.out* and typed *del **. As a result, the student erased all of the files (editors, compilers, student files, etc.) on the entire machine.

- Workers in one large company all wore identification badges for security reasons. When the operator for a large computer system was changing a disk, however, he was unaware that his badge accidentally had fallen into the drive where the new disk was mounted. When he started up the disk, the badge was thrown at high speed into various parts of the disk and drive, ruining both and destroying thousands of company records.

  The resulting situation had both good and bad news. The good news was that the company maintained a backup disk with duplicate data in case something happened to a disk in use. The bad news was that after realizing the first disk had been destroyed, the operator decided to correct the problem by mounting the backup disk on the same drive. When the drive was restarted this second time, the backup disk suffered the same fate as the original one.

- At the North American Aerospace Defence Command (NORAD), simulations included scenarios involving enemy attacks, and appropriate data were available on tape to conduct such simulation exercises. On November 9, 1979, following such a simulation, an operator accidentally failed to remove such a simulation tape from a drive that usually was used for a backup copy of normal system data. Subsequently, the main system failed, this simulation tape was read, and missiles appeared on system screens, causing an alert for six minutes until the problem could be identified. (In that time, 10 tactical fighters were launched from bases in the northern United States and Canada.)[2]

While well-trained operators normally can be particularly helpful in maintaining a smoothly running computer operation, a single mistake can have rather sweeping consequences.

TECHNIQUES TO REDUCE HUMAN ERROR

Since human error can have significant consequences in entering data and operating computer systems, a variety of techniques have been developed to help reduce the likelihood of such errors or to protect a system when such problems arise. Chapter 5 reviewed the use of check digits to help identify errors, and the first part of this chapter mentioned checking information as it is entered. Such review of data can identify some types of errors and question unlikely data values. At a higher level, some techniques involve the use of more sophisticated analysis of input and the development of dialogues between computers and people to identify and review data or processing steps. In addition, automation sometimes can eliminate the need for some input.

User-Computer Interfaces. Machines and programs may vary considerably on how people are expected to enter data. For example, computer users may press keys or move arrows (using a mouse) or touch screens. There is also considerable variation concerning the format of data and the care required to enter data correctly. The appearance of data on terminals or paper and the activities people perform to enter data are all part of the **user–computer interface**. When this interface is designed carefully, data may be typed quickly, proofreading is straightforward, and correction of errors is accomplished easily. In contrast, poor interfaces may be extremely tedious and error-prone, and review and correction of data may require considerable patience and expertise. In short, some interfaces may aid users in entering data correctly, while others may encourage difficulties. Some examples illustrate both of these extremes.

- When computers used punched cards for entering data, the first card of each task, called a *JOB* card, often gave accounting information as well as a list of parameters about how the job should be handled. In particular, the user could supply up to five parameters, separated by commas. For example, at one facility, the card

  ```
  //JOB (200,3,314150,453,TEST),WALKER
  ```

  might be deciphered as follows: Project (or account number) 314150 will be billed for computer time, and the name of the user is WALKER. This specific task may run up to 200 time units, it will require special resources (3 = special paper and a special disk), and the monthly bill will show this as job 453 with the name TEST. Of these parameters, only the project number and the user name were required; the other data were optional. Data were omitted by leaving the space between commas blank, although commas were required as place holders when later fields were to be specified. Thus, a simplified JOB card that listed only the project number, user, and billing job number would be

  ```
  //JOB (,,314150,453),WALKER
  ```

  Omitting the first comma would change the run to account 453 and require unusual special services (following code 314150).

  With such a sequence of commas, etc., such cards were often incorrectly typed and a steady source of frustration. (At some computer facilities, the sequence of commas could be much longer than shown here, and the possibilities for error were correspondingly increased.)

- In contrast, a recent database package was designed to store names, addresses, and other information on members of a community development foundation. When a user enters or updates data for a member, the screen appears with places for each possible piece of information, these places are logically labeled, and the user uses a mouse or keyboard arrows to move from one field to another. This interface allows all of the data to be reviewed and corrected easily.

- On the machine level, some equipment has many rows of identical switches or knobs that can be turned to many positions. In working with such equipment, it is very easy to push the wrong switch or to be off by one position in setting a knob. For example, the climate control for the 1985 Dodge Caravan contains six identical push buttons, labeled *off, vent, bi-level vent, heat, defrost,* and *max ac.* Since these are located diagonally under the steering wheel, it is difficult for the driver to locate the correct one while the car is moving. (In fact, the display is even more confusing, in that both the *vent* and *bi-level* buttons can be pushed in for air conditioning or pushed and then pulled out for air flow without air conditioning. When pulled out, there is no visual clue as to whether *vent* or *bi-level* settings are in use.) The reader might also have noticed that many high-fidelity amplifiers have a similar feature of many identical buttons. When used on stereo equipment, such controls may be annoying, but they are unlikely to cause damage. In cars, such controls may distract a driver. In aircraft or nuclear reactors, clearly, the risks from such controls would be much higher.

• In contrast, people are less likely to confuse switches with different colors and shapes.

Artificial Intelligence and Expert Systems. With the possibilities

for human error in entering data or operating systems, software designers often try to minimize the consequences of such problems. In general, this anticipation of errors may take two basic forms. First, software may analyze data as they are received to detect errors and then take action to obtain corrected information. Second, processing itself may allow for the possibility that input information may contain mistakes or inconsistencies.

One general approach for accomplishing these tasks involves the use of rules to reach conclusions. This use of rules in solving problems represents one important approach investigated within the branch of computer science, called **artificial intelligence**, and the resulting programs are called **expert systems**.

Example: Snakes in Texas – One simple program of this type identifies snakes in the state of Texas.[3] In this program, a typical rule states (in coded form)

Rule 05:
If the color of the snake is either grey or brown,
   And the size of the snake is small,
   And the snake has a ring around its neck
Then there is an 80% chance that the snake is a prairie ringneck.
Another rule states
Rule 05a:
If the snake is a prairie ringneck,
Then the snake's Latin name is "Diadophis punctatus arnyi."
This program also has several rules to identify which Texas snakes are poisonous.

In running this program, the machine asks various questions and makes inferences about several characteristics of a snake and about its identity, following the rules given. In this process, since conclusions depend upon various certainty factors or likelihoods that a conclusion follows, some reasonable conclusions can be based on uncertain or erroneous data. For example, Professor Gordon S. Novak, Jr., Director of the Artificial Intelligence Laboratory at the University of Texas at Austin, has described using the system to identify the snake observed by someone who called Professor Novak with some information. In this case, the description of the snake (seen in the Austin area) did not match that of any actual snake. However, the program could conclude that the snake was not poisonous, since the snake did not have match any descriptions of any poisonous snakes that live in Texas. (Such a conclusion might be drawn, for example, for a green and yellow, striped snake of medium size that had no rattles on its tail.) Here, the program failed to specify the actual name of the snake – perhaps the caller made a mistake in observing the snake as it moved under plantings through a garden. Snakes of the given description do not exist in Texas. On the other hand, the program did address a major question in the caller's mind – the snake was not poisonous.

More generally, these rule-based systems have several helpful properties. First, the programs themselves generally are reasonably simple. Much of the processing depends upon rules, which are stored as data. The use of the rules follow straightforward algorithms, and the programs can be rather short. Second, since rule-based programs are often reasonably short and simple, there are relatively few difficulties in writing, testing, and correcting programming errors. In normal use, the programs themselves have few errors. Third, while the data for these systems involve a large number of rules, these rules normally can be expressed in a form that is understandable by experts in the field. For example, the rules listed earlier for the identification of snakes are stated in a natural form (at least for people who know something about snakes in Texas). Fourth, most rule-based systems allow users to print out the chain of inferences and rules involved in reaching specific conclusions. This allows a review of the decision-making process. Finally, the use of probabilities (often called **confidence factors**) may allow several pieces of data to outweigh one inconsistent piece. A program sometimes may downplay an incorrect piece of data in favor of several consistent, correct ones. Each of these properties may help identify likely sources of data error and may facilitate making a variety of conclusions. The rules can help analyze input data, leading to the identification of a wide range of possible data entry errors.

On the other hand, while these properties can be very useful in developing programs, rule-based systems also have some of the limitations shared by other types of programs. For example, these programs depend upon the correctness and the completeness of specifications. In the context of rule-based systems, reliance upon correctness and completeness carries over to the data as well, since all conclusions depend upon the rules that are specified. In the snakes example, the validity of rule 05 depends upon the assertion that a small, grey or brown snake with a ring around its neck is a prairie ringneck. All of these characteristics must be consistent with this type of snake, and this must be enough information to distinguish prairie ringnecks from other snakes. Later in that program, the rules assert that the poisonous snakes in Texas are rattlesnakes, Texas coral snakes, water moccasins, and copperheads, and that information formed the basis for the earlier illustration that a green and yellow, striped snake of medium size that had no rattles on its tail was not poisonous. According to the logic, the observed snake was none of the poisonous snakes on the list, so it could not have been poisonous. Such a conclusion clearly depends upon the completeness and correctness of the poisonous snake list. As a practical matter, people often assume the "obvious" in stating rules, but such details are rarely so obvious to a computer. In proofreading rules, people therefore often make simple assumptions, and rules that seem complete can yield unexpected conclusions. As a result, identifying a proper set of hypotheses for a rule can be particularly difficult.

Other, more subtle issues about the effectiveness of expert systems arise from the order of the rules given and upon the use of probabilities or confidence factors. Rule-based systems do have some worthwhile characteristics, but they do not resolve many of the fundamental difficulties of software. Issues may move from programming problems in traditional programs to questions about data, but the basic difficulties remain.

Automated Tools. Another approach to avoiding human errors involves the automation of some steps in the problem-solving process, so that people will not have the opportunity to make mistakes. One extreme of this view was illustrated in the movie *2001: A Space Odyssey*, where the computer Hal communicates with people though speech. Hal understands what people say (in one case, Hal even reads lips), and Hal responds to the problems asked. In this view, a person identifies a problem, an interaction with the computer clarifies the request, and the computer does the required work. At this stage of automation, a person cannot make data entry errors, since the entire data gathering process is automated.

Such an extreme, of course, is well beyond today's capacities of computing. The technical issues involved just with understanding speech are formidable, and there is little reason to believe that general dialogues between people and machines will be possible for many years.[4] Similarly, the successful computer systems of today focus on specific needs and applications; no software has sufficient flexibility to respond to a wide range of needs involving many applications.

Automated Code Generation – While the extreme represented by Hal may exist only in the movies, active research continues in several limited fields. Two such areas involve automated code generation and automated verification. Automated code generation attempts to translate specifications or algorithms directly into code. This approach depends upon the perspective that if the requirements of a problem can be specified clearly and precisely enough, then the work of producing actual code may be relatively straightforward. In this work, the development of requirements or algorithms already addresses such issues as completeness, correctness, and feasibility. Automated code generation would eliminate human error as algorithms were translated into code, but it would assume that the algorithms were correct initially.

At some levels, the automation of this translation process can be (and already is) quite successful. When algorithms are written in a high-level, formal language, such as Pascal, Ada, FORTRAN, or COBOL, compilers are available to translate these algorithms into a machine language that will run directly on a variety of machines. Some programs also successfully translate from one computer language (e.g., FORTRAN) to another (e.g., Ada). In each of these cases, the translation usually depends upon the precision of the statement of the original algorithm. Algorithms written in a programming language are carefully expressed, there is little opportunity for ambiguity, and rules of syntax are precisely known. All of these characteristics combine to make this level of translation practical.

With less formal languages, however, many difficulties may arise. English is notoriously ambiguous, for example. (In an early experiment in language translation, a program was asked to translate the saying "the spirit is willing but the flesh is weak" into Russian. Another program took the result, translated it back to English, and produced the result "the liquor is okay but the meat has gone bad." Another example in the folklore involving English–French translation started with the expression "Out of sight, out of mind" and produced the result "Blind, insane.")[5] English idioms, alternate meanings, and ambiguous syntax complicate the meaning of natural language statements considerably.

Another range of problems arise when algorithms are to be implemented on a system of processors in a distributed network. Frequently algorithms are designed for specific configurations of machines. For example, work by Chandy and Misra[6] provides a general language for specifying parallel algorithms for use on various distributed systems. Algorithms can be constructed and proven correct whenever they are implemented, and a powerful framework is available for thinking about parallel machines. However, the translation of algorithms in this language to various machines currently requires additional constraints and special properties. At present there is little reason to expect the automatic, effective translation of algorithms in this language to efficient programs that can be run on various architectures. Similar restrictions normally apply to other research activities in this area.[7] Parallel algorithms can be written, discussed, and verified at a high level, but the translation seems to require a special step to take advantage of special constraints placed on the logical expressions.

In general, automatic translation currently seems to be a reasonable possibility when language is constrained, when meanings can be inferred easily, and when algorithms are to be run on a single processor. This suggests that automatic code generation may be possible when single-processor algorithms can be specified in a formal manner, either in a formal English or mathematical style or in a programming language. For example, many high-level translators (often called **compilers** and **interpreters**) already exist. As the range of expressions and meanings increases or the number of processors goes up, however, algorithms for translation become harder to specify, and the likelihood of effective machine translation decreases. Only special cases are possible now, although more general approaches may be developed in the coming years. On the other hand, there is little reason to expect computers to generate code when specifications or algorithms are incomplete or imprecise. The form for specifications may not be a critical issue, but precision and completeness certainly are vital.

Automated Verification – Another approach to eliminating human errors in coding algorithms involves proving that a code segment performs the job intended. Specifically, one develops a mathematical proof that a piece of code meets its specifications. Such an approach may or may not help in constructing the code in the first place, but in any case, trying to prove correctness can help identify errors.

This process of proving correctness begins by writing in a formal, mathematical notation what can be assumed at the start of a piece of code and what is to be true at the end. Such statements are called **preconditions** and **postconditions**, respectively. A proof then consists of applying specified rules of logic to each step of a program to show that given the preconditions, the statements of the program lead to the postconditions.

For many program elements, such logical deductions can be made in a rather straightforward way. Steps are reasonably mechanical, and rules are reasonably easy to apply. However, one programming construct presents more problems, and this construct, called a **loop**, involves telling a computer to repeat a series of instructions. In handling loops, it may be extremely difficult to take advantage of formal rules of inference, and the normal proof technique is to identify conditions that should hold each time the series of instructions is begun. Such conditions are called **loop invariants.** In adding many numbers, for example, a variable *total* always might be the sum of the numbers processed so far. As more numbers are considered, *total* is changed to reflect the new sum. Such loop invariants clarify how loops behave, and they are vital in proving that loops meet their specifications. In fact, in many cases, given a program segment with preconditions, postconditions, and loop invariants, it is a completely mechanical process to prove that the code meets its specifications. Programs can be written to perform this task, at least in certain circumstances, and the correctness of a code segment may be verified mechanically.

Unfortunately, the identification of loop invariants is still an art. The invariants must be strong enough to prove that the desired postconditions will be true when the loop is finished, but they must also be weak enough so that they can be assured by the preconditions. Since they also give information about how a loop functions, they may need to include properties about the loop itself. As a result, people currently have little idea about how to specify rules for finding loop invariants, and there is little prospect of automating this part of the proof process for some time.

With loop invariants specified, automatic code verification may have the potential to check code mechanically, as long as specifications are written formally and with sufficient care, and such verification could have a substantial impact in finding some types of errors. (Errors in specifications might still exist, but verification could find additional errors made in coding.) Unfortunately, without a statement of all loop invariants, automatic code verification is well beyond current capabilities and understandings.

══ OTHER ISSUES ══

So far this chapter has followed a familiar form in the application of technology. It began with an identification of a problem: people can make mistakes in running computer systems, and these mistakes can have serious consequences. Next, the chapter identified some ways technology itself could be used to help resolve these problems: for example, user–computer interfaces can be made more natural, easier to proofread, and simpler to correct; machines can be made more sophisticated in reviewing input and making decisions; and some operations can be automated to eliminate the need for human interference (with a corresponding reduction in the chance of human error).

Unfortunately, as is often the case, such technological solutions themselves can present new problems and challenges, some of which can be rather subtle.

Acceptance of Computer-Generated Results. People often accept information and actions of computer systems without great analysis. People sometimes demonstrate a blind faith in technology; there may be a sense that whatever the computer does must be right. For example, when this author was in college, he received the monthly telephone bill, divided the calls among six roommates, and computed each person's bill. For the first two months of this process, the author did all such work by hand, and handwritten bills were distributed. In each case, the bill was reviewed by each roommate, and questions frequently arose. Later, since the amounts of the monthly bills were considerable, the author wrote a computer program to tabulate and print bills for each roommate. Thereafter, no roommate ever challenged any bill, even though the computer mimicked the manual processes.

In other cases, regular users of a computer system frequently come to expect it to react consistently in certain ways. When a system normally gives correct and accurate information, people often accept new results with little review. Since outcomes have been correct in the past, people expect new results to be similar.

In each of these cases, the fact that a computer produced the output seems to validate the results. Further, the fancier or more elegant the presentation (with graphics or elegant fonts), the more the output presents the image of professionalism, and the more likely people are to accept the conclusions.

Of course, the impact of nicely designed materials has been known for a long time. (In the October 31, 1989 comic strip *Calvin and Hobbs*, for example, Calvin once expected a particularly good grade when he turned in a science project in a "professional clear plastic binder." In one actual high school known to this author, students report that the combination of a nice looking title page with the use of such a binder typically increased the outcome of a project by about half a grade.)

With the capabilities of today's computers and modern desktop publishing packages, professional results can be produced reasonably easily, and the quality of content might bear no relationship to the quality of the graphics and visual images. Further, with the use of word processors to produce both preliminary and final versions of reports, rough drafts can look particularly elegant. Many people report that they have difficulty getting feedback on a first version of a paper or on an initial outline when the output has a professional appearance. In some cases, perhaps, reviewers do not want to deface what they see; in other cases, the look of the paper may give it additional authority or credibility.

More generally, computer graphics and other computer-generated output can change people's perception of reality, so that the model generated by the computer may be taken as true without validity checks that people are accustomed to making in other contexts.

Complexity. In a separate issue, many attempts to reduce the possibility of human error in computer systems involve increasing the sophistication of hardware and software to check user input and to provide more easily understood user–computer interfaces. While these approaches certainly can help detect and correct mistakes, these same attempts also can greatly increase the complexity of computer systems, and such complexity is a major source of software error. Simple input and output may be cumbersome for the user, but they are often rather straightforward to program. Short, simple specifications often lead to programs with few subtleties.

In contrast, software with extensive specifications and sophisticated error checking often involves many separate sections or modules of code, where each module many involve complex logic, and where there may be extensive interactions among modules. Such software is far from being straightforward, and the possibilities for error can be rather extensive. Testing often cannot cover all possible interactions, and the likelihood of error may be rather high.

This risk of hardware or software error, therefore, raises a difficult problem for system designers. Any system provides many opportunities for human error in the running of the system, and it is reasonable to design hardware and software to check the actions of users and operators to guard against such difficulties. On the other hand, the addition of error avoidance and error checking capabilities may increase system complexity significantly, raising the likelihood that the system itself will contain design or coding errors. When such mistakes do occur, users and operators need special capabilities to make corrections, often bypassing the error-checking processes that made the mistakes in the first place.

Circumventing Checking Procedures. When procedures are developed to identify and resolve errors, it seems trite to note that the procedures will only work if they are used. Unfortunately, people tend to avoid extra steps and annoying details when they can, so their jobs can be accomplished more easily or more quickly. As a simple example, a massive amount of data shows that the use of seat belts can help prevent death or serious injury in automobiles, and yet many people choose not to wear their belts. Further, when cars are designed to monitor the use of seat belts by ringing buzzers or failing to start when belts are not connected, such alarms are routinely circumvented by sitting on previously buckled belts or by removing the sensors or alarms. When people do not want to use the seat belts, they will find a way to avoid these safety devices.

Similarly, computer systems may contain checks of user input or processing. Unusual or incorrect conditions may be identified, but users may chose to ignore, avoid, or turn off warnings and alarms. On some computer systems, for example, the machines normally ask the user to confirm his or her intentions whenever one or more files are to be deleted. This allows the user to review the names of files being discarded and to retain data that were identified incorrectly. On the other hand, when many data files are to be removed, users may find it tedious to confirm the deletion of each one, and such systems may allow the disabling of the confirmation mode. As a result, the user has no mechanism to correct typographical errors before data are lost.

In one recent spectacular case in a beginning programming class, a student wanted to remove a file named *prog?.p* . Since this file was the only one with a question mark in the name, the user typed *remove *?**, since the character * represented any combination of characters. From this student's perspective, the command would delete any information in files that contained any number of characters before or after a question mark. Since the given file was the only one with a question mark, this file would be identified. Unfortunately, on that machine, the question mark represented any single letter when used within a file name, so the symbols **?** translated to any name with at least one character. Thus, the command actually issued removed all files in the student's account. In this situation, the good news was that the system normally asked for confirmation for each file being deleted. The bad news was that this student had become tired of the tedium of responding affirmatively for each file, so the student had disabled this checking process. As a result, a semester's worth of work was eliminated within a few seconds. (One might ask if the student had followed standard procedures by making backup copies of the data disk prior to this session of work, but the reader probably can anticipate the unfortunate answer to this second example of following procedures.)

Similar horror stories abound within the computer community. Safeguard procedures for data always require that multiple copies be available, and that these data be stored in separate locations (normally in separate buildings). Then if one copy of data is destroyed or corrupted, another copy will be available. Such procedures, of course, are only useful if they are consistently and conscientiously applied. (In one actual case, a duplicate copy of a data disk was carefully made and stored separately, but to prevent it from becoming lost, the user used a thumb tack to secure the disk to a bulletin board.)

Likewise, when computers control other machinery, experiments, or processes, users must continually monitor the system for possible difficulties, and operators must respond when warnings are reported. Clearly developed procedures can guide users in resolving the problems, but the effectiveness of the response depends upon the willingness, training, and ability of users to follow those procedures. When procedures, controls, or warnings are ignored, systems may fail with particularly serious consequences. For example, some of the difficulties leading to the Chernobyl disaster involved circumventing procedures and ignoring warnings. Safety checks and procedures may require time and care, but system integrity may depend upon the faithful adherence of all users to such details.

Compounding of Errors.   Once something does go wrong within a computer system, resolution of the problem normally depends upon appropriate backup systems or procedures. When one error, one discrepancy, or one system failure has occurred, the solution frequently uses other system components or capabilities. In complex systems, plans may even include procedures for handling multiple failures, although clearly any corrective action depends upon something working properly.

Extreme difficulties arise when the pattern of failures extends beyond anticipated scenarios, making planned procedures and backup systems ineffective. Such multiple failures can arise in two basic ways: several independent errors or failures may occur at approximately the same time, or the failure of one component or system may affect the function of several others.

Multiple Independent Failures – In the first case, several components may fail simultaneously, or the improper functioning of some parts may not be repaired before other parts also fail. Such difficulties may be compounded when human operators respond improperly. While such circumstances may seem improbable, they do occur. For example, on May 24, 1986, a front page story in the *Washington Post* reported the following concerning an emergency shutdown at the Davis-Besse Nuclear Power Plant.

> For ... 29 minutes, experts say, Davis-Besse came as close to a meltdown as any U. S. nuclear plant since the Three Mile Island accident of 1979. Faced with a loss of water to cool the reactor and the improbable breakdown of 14 separate components, operators performed a rescue mission noted both for skill and human foible: They pushed wrong buttons, leaped down steep stairs, wended their way through a maze of locked chambers and finally saved the day last June 9 by muscling free the valves and plugging fuses into a small, manually operated pump not designed for emergency. It resupplied water to the overheating system temporarily, allowing technicians to restore the plant's normal safety mechanism. [8]

At nuclear power plants, one would expect contingency plans to anticipate multiple failures, and training would cover a very wide range of contingencies. However, the failure of *fourteen separate components* certainly is beyond any reasonable expectation, and yet it happened.

As a second example, on August 16, 1989, trading on the Toronto Stock Exchange was halted for almost three hours when both the primary and backup disk drive systems failed. Apparently, three separate failures were responsible for the problems. Here, the computer system was specially designed with ample redundancy, so that operation could continue when any piece of hardware failed, and there was every reason to expect that prompt attention to one failure would repair that problem before another malfunction occurred. In this case, however, three failures knocked out the primary database for many stocks, and most operations on the Stock Exchange were halted. (Other computer operations could continue, and stock information stored on another disk system remained available. Without access to the primary database, however, the functioning of other components of the system was inadequate.)

According to John Kane, vice-president for marketing strategy for Tandem Computers of Canada, the system vendor involved, "Fault-tolerance guarantees that you will not have a problem from any single failure, . . . I've never heard of three failures at one time. I don't know what the gods were doing to us."[9]

Redundant systems, sometime called **fault-tolerant systems**, can guarantee that they will continue to function properly when any single failure occurs. They cannot, however, guarantee uninterrupted service when several parts fail. While such multiple independent failures do not occur every day, they do arise with some frequency, and the possibility of them happening should not be overlooked.

Failures in Linked Systems – While multiple failures do happen occasionally when components are independent, the frequency of failure can be dramatically higher when components are linked in some way. A particularly clear case was reported by Chuck Weinstock.[10]

> I have heard stores about pilots following the procedures in the manual, but not being able to save the aircraft. In the case of the American Airlines DC-10 accident, the pilot executed the correct maneuver for loss of engine power, but the effects of the missing engine caused it to go into a stall. However, the correction for the stall is 180 degrees different from the correction for the loss of engine power, and thus the plane was lost. The pilot could have saved the aircraft had he known what was going on. The reason the pilot didn't correct for the stall is that he didn't know about it (or knew too late) – because the missing engine supplied power to the stall warning device.

When one component powers or controls another, clearly a failure in the first leads to failure in the second. Even when components seem logically separate, however, physical connections or relationships can tie them together. For example, in the *Washington Post* of June 4, 1986, Jack Anderson and Dale Van Atta reported the following.

> Incredibly, the new guidelines [of the Nuclear Regulatory Commission] let nuclear plant operators sidestep the protection of redundant control systems by planning fire safety for the first set of controls only.
>
> The guidelines permit partial fire barriers between the first control system and the backup system, which can be in the same room. This means that a fire could short-circuit both systems.[11]

Similar difficulties can arise in a wide variety of ways. For example, the communications for separate systems pass through the same conduit, so that rupturing the ducting could affect multiple systems. To be truly effective, redundant systems must be both logically and physically separate, so one can fail at any point without any effect upon the others. One accident or mishap may affect one component or system, but robust systems must guard against such problems affecting multiple systems. There will always be some chance that multiple failures may occur when systems are independent, but such chances are enhanced considerably whenever the systems are linked even in subtle ways.

Reliability of Error Recovery Code. When systems do fail or when discrepancies or errors are found, the normal expectation is that procedures, hardware, and software can be used to resolve the problem. Specifically, one expects that software will work properly in meeting the conditions it was designed to handle. While such expectations may be appropriate, it is worthwhile to ask how one knows that such software will work when needed. Chapters 6 and 7 have noted, for example, that the reliability of many large software systems depends upon testing and use. The more a piece of code is exercised, the more different conditions it will meet, and the more likely that any errors will be found. Frequently used code is regularly subjected to demanding testing as part of its normal operation, and over the course of time the code will experience a wide range of cases and circumstances.

In contrast, seldom used code is not faced with constant tests and new situations as part of its normal operation. Special tests may be constructed and run to give some level of assurance that the code works properly, but it is rare that the range of work on special procedures includes the variety of circumstances that is found for code that handles normal processing. Daily operations naturally test the software that handles common events, but normal operation does not frequently use the software needed to identify and resolve errors.

While this observation is hardly revolutionary, it does imply that software for exception handling is likely to be subjected to less testing and is therefore likely to contain more errors than frequently used code. Thus, when systems do fail, the corrective actions often use the least reliable software available, and the most critical work of resolving errors and failures is often left to the software that has been used the least. Similar comments amply to procedures used in error recovery and to the training and experience of operators and users. Since resolution of problems normally happens relatively infrequently, this work will involve the least tested procedures, and it will be performed by people whose training may have covered these areas least.

Thus, while failures and errors can occur in many ways, the resolution of such problems often involves the least tested software and procedures. Further, the more infrequently a situation arises, the less testing can be expected, and the less experience by personnel. When situations are critical, the correction of errors and failures may actually involve the weakest part of a system's operation.

═══ SUMMARY ═══

Many of the issues discussed in this chapter come together in some explanations concerning the Korean Air Lines Flight 007 that flew over the Soviet Union and was shot down on September 1, 1983. While no one knows precisely what led the flight to stray off its planned route and over Soviet air space, several proposed scenarios involve points made here.

1. On the Boeing 747 used for Flight 007, the means of navigation were selected by a five-position Auto Pilot Selector Switch. Of these five positions, the first two adjacent options were called *INS* (using the plane's Internal Navigation System) and *HDG* (following a specified compass heading). The path of Flight 007 was completely consistent with using magnetic heading 246 degrees rather than the INS flight plan charted by the pilot. Thus, one reasonable explanation of the plane's actual flight could be simple human error; the Selector Switch was set to *HDG* rather than the adjacent position *INS*. The switch itself was not internally lit, it was not easily visible, and there was no need for a pilot or copilot to work with it once it was set. While such mistakes are not common, flight records suggest that such mistakes do occur from time to time. Further, the layout and dark location of the controls make it rather unlikely that the mistake would be detected directly.[12]

2. A second scenario involves several human and design flaws.[13]
   - In preparing for the flight, the flight engineer incorrectly entered the runway ramp position into the first of the three INS systems as W139 degrees longitude rather than W149 degrees. This was a simple typographical error.
   - When the position was entered into a second INS system, an error noting the discrepancy was automatically reported. The flight engineer had faith in the first INS system as originally programmed and assumed that the error was in the second system.
   - A single touch of a button cleared the light warning of the discrepancy, eliminating the problem from the perspective of the flight engineer.

- When the position was entered into the third INS system, no error was reported, since the previous clearing of the second system turned off all further warnings of discrepancies or errors.
- While the pilot and copilot are supposed to check original work by the flight engineer, this was omitted.
- The "daily maintenance report" for the previous flight of this aircraft indicated two malfunctions. First, while the copilot's horizontal situation indicator normally shows if the plane is being flown using a magnetic heading setting, this indicator was not working. Second, the warning light telling of such a malfunction was out.
- Since dignitaries were aboard the plane, the pilot was expected to spend time away from the cockpit during the flight chatting with these people. Thus, responsibility for the flight fell to the copilot, whose horizontal situation indicator was malfunctioning.

As with the first scenario, each event described here is consistent with observed behavior. Errors are made entering data, and people forget to check the work of others. Further, a single button was available to turn off all warnings of discrepancies among the triply redundant INS systems on the plane, pilots often do use the clear button rather than reprogramming the entire system, and multiple (but seemingly minor) hardware malfunctions had occurred.

In each case, cumbersome or flawed design coupled with simple human error to introduce an incorrect flight path into the plane's navigation system. In addition, other known malfunctions and circumstances allowed the flight to continue without prompting the crew to detect these errors.

═══ CONCLUSIONS AND IMPLICATIONS ═══

In the course of their work, people naturally make mistakes. One can expect errors within the work of even the most careful individuals, so it is inevitable that people using or operating computers will make their share. Errors may range from simple typographical or procedural errors to sophisticated, multistep problems that accumulate over some period of time. Regardless of the best intentions, errors will always be part of any computing environment. The issue for designing and operating computer systems, therefore, is not whether such problems will arise. They will. Rather, the issue is what should happen when things go wrong.

Unfortunately, the course of action to handle errors and failures is not always very clear. On the one hand, computers can be programmed to check the input of data, to monitor the actions of computer operators, and to search for discrepancies in processing. Further, user–computer interfaces may be made more readable to encourage users to proofread and correct their work. All of these approaches automate the error detection and correction process, and all can be effective.

On the other hand, as the computer performs more monitoring of data entry and processing, the controlling software becomes more sophisticated, and the likelihood of software error increases. Techniques in artificial intelligence and expert systems may be added, but the common issues of completeness and correctness still arise. Further, even if monitoring techniques are very advanced, there will still be a need for people to correct specific problems when they arise, so capabilities must be present to allow people to meddle with the internal parts of a system.

Overall, then, every system must strive for a careful balance between the automation and computer checking of users and operators and the human checking and correction of computer systems. Errors can arise with either people or machines, and both may need to monitor and correct the other.

The reaching of this balance is complicated by several other issues. People tend to accept conclusions displayed by computers, and the more elegant or slick the presentation, the more people may be willing to accept the result. To help with such problems, procedures are needed to review output critically and to correct errors as needed. Another common human trait, however, involves looking for shortcuts or trying to find easier ways to perform a job. In some cases, procedures may not be followed properly, even when they are carefully developed. The resolution of errors and system failures may be further compounded when several components fail at once or when problems are found in seldom-used error-recovery procedures and software.

The history of computing is filled with examples of people making a variety of errors and of those mistakes being compounded by further errors in software or human responses. With the range of possibilities for human error and with the inventiveness people show in creating new scenarios, one must expect that similar human errors will always be a part of any system. Error-free operation of any complex computer system over a long period of time is particularly unlikely.

═══ DISCUSSION QUESTIONS ═══

8.1 Describe some practical ways to resolve data entry errors.

8.2 Suppose a computer is to be designed to monitor prices entered by clerks in a grocery store.

a. When should the computer reject the cost of a grocery item?

b. Should the computer require a clerk to verify that a value previously entered is actually correct? If a cost is possible, but unlikely, how should the computer react?

8.3 One grocery store, which used scanners to identify items being purchased, has the following policies:

- A clerk must call a manager to insert a key every time amounts over $50 must be entered.

- Customers are told that they will received an item free if the price quoted on the shelves differs from that charged at the checkout register.

How might these policies help the store handle issues of human error?

8.4 Review the two scenarios that led to Korean Airlines Flight 007 to be significantly off course over Soviet air space. Identify both the errors that might have occurred and instances of poor design. How could procedures be changed or designs modified to resolve these problems?

8.5 Korean Airlines Flight 007 used triply redundant INS units manufactured by Litton Aero Products. Data were entered independently into each of these units, so that data entry errors could be detected. Then, when a comparison of the data or computations in the three units noted any discrepancies, a warning light was activated.

a. Discuss the advantages and disadvantages of having such redundant systems. What errors would you expect to be caught by such systems? What errors could not be caught?

b. Discuss the wisdom of including a "clear" button, which deactivates the warning system for such redundant systems.

c. In the case of Flight 007, one INS unit actually controlled the plane; the other units acted as a check for the first one. Discuss the advantages and disadvantages of such a configuration.

8.6 If a meter reader, going house to house, is responsible both for reading the meter and for entering the data into a machine that can be plugged directly into a central computer system, what safeguards might be considered to ensure that the readings and typing are done correctly? E.g., how might you design procedures or recording equipment to minimize the likelihood that the data entered by the meter reader would be incorrect?

8.7 Approximately 10% of males are color blind.

    a. What implications does this have in an environment that is increasingly reliant on color images?

    b. Where should system developers be careful in the use of color to convey messages?

8.8 This chapter notes that once loop invariants are determined, it is possible to determine mechanically (following specific rules) when a program will produce the correct answers, required by its specifications. Since part of this process includes determining whether a program will terminate, it would seem that a determination of such loop invariants could be used to decide whether a program would ever stop. On the other hand, Chapter 3 proved that the Halting Problem was unsolvable. Discuss what conclusions you can draw from these observations? Are there open questions that need to be resolved? What can you say about the future for automated verification techniques?

8.9 Why do computers need human interaction at all? Describe some possible advantages or disadvantages of a future world where those things that now require human intervention are automated.

NOTES

1   Reported by *The Daily Spectrum,* St. George, Utah, on August 21, 1989 and circulated in *Software Engineering Notes*, Volume 14, Number 6, October 1989, p. 3.

2   Reported in *Software Engineering Notes*, Volume 5, Number 3, November 1979 and in David Bellin and Gary Chapman, *Computers in Battle*, Harcourt Brace Javanovich, New York, 1987, pp. 16, 106.

3   This program was written by Professor Gordon Novak, Director of the Artificial Intelligence Laboratory at the University of Texas at Austin. For more information, see Gordon S. Novak, Jr., *TMYCIN Expert System Tool*, Report AI87-52, written April 1987 and revised August 1988 for the Artificial Intelligence Laboratory, the University of Texas at Austin.

4   Currently, some computer systems can recognize speech using a very limited vocabulary (perhaps 100 words). The approach breaks speech into various sound patterns and then matches the patterns with words. While the details are quite complex and beyond the scope of this discussion, such pattern recognition problems are subject to the combinatorial explosion problem described in Chapter 4. Professor Gordon Novak, Director of the Artificial Intelligence Laboratory at the University of Texas at Austin, has noted, for example, that

many attempts have been made to recognize a few words. However, researchers have never been successful in scaling these systems up greatly. Systems that work reasonably for a few (hundred) words fail miserably when they have to handle a few thousand words. Either messages involving a large vocabulary take much too long to process to be feasible or such systems cannot distinguish words in a reasonable way.

5   Reported by Karla Jennings in *The Devouring Fungus*, W. W. Norton, New York, 1990, pp. 93–94. This source also states that when the same Russian–English double translation experiment cited previously was given "Out of sight, out of mind," the resulting English was, "Invisible idiot."

6   See K. Mani Chandy and Jayadev Misra, *Parallel Program Design: A Foundation*, Addison-Wesley, Reading, Massachusetts, 1988.

7   See, for example, the work of Leslie Lamport, who writes parallel algorithms using formal mathematical constructs, called *temporal logic*.

8   Michael Weisskopf, "Ohio Nuclear Plant Mishap Raises Questions on U. S. Safety," *The Washington Post*, May 24, 1986, p. 1.

9   Reported by Geoffrey Rowan, "TSE Seeking to Prevent Further Computer Chaos," *Globe and Mail*, August 21, 1989, p. B–1.

10   Reported in *Software Enginering Notes*, Volume 11, Number 5, October 1986, p. 7

11   Jack Anderson and Dale Van Atta, "U. S. Atom Plants Have Unique Hazards," *The Washington Post*, June 4, 1986, p. E24.

12   Additional arguments for this explanation of Flight 007's route may be found in Murray Sayle, "KE007: A Conspiracy of Circumstance," *The New York Review of Books*, April 25, 1985, pp. 44–54. This article also notes additional hardware failures and human factors that may have contributed to the failure of the crew to detect the error once it was made.

13   This scenario was developed by Harold Ewing and the International Civic Air Organization (ICO). For more details, see Seymour M. Hirsh, "The Target Is Destroyed," Random House, Inc., New York, 1986.

CHAPTER **9**

"Forget straw-into-gold, I just put a cool million in your bank account."

Security Issues

Back in the misty eons of time (perhaps even as recently as fifty or one hundred years ago), security for vital or sensitive information was a relatively straightforward matter. Within a company, for example, data might be collected and tabulated on paper, organized into folders and file drawers, protected by fireproof vaults, and monitored by police patrols and guards. Such measures ensured that authorized personnel could work with the data, but personal or sensitive information could not circulate.

In this context, primary difficulties with the limited distribution and availability of information might be divided into three categories:

- *Physical Threats:* Files might be damaged or destroyed by physical means, such as fire or water.

- *Insiders:* People within the company, employees with authorization to work with the data, might copy or memorize information and bring it away for outside circulation.

- *Outsiders:* People outside the company might physically break into buildings and files.

To protect against such problems, vaults might be built fireproof, waterproof, etc.; backgrounds of workers might be checked and monitored; and security police might patrol. Special procedures limiting access to data and the movement of documents might supply further protection.

At a basic level, computer security includes these same traditional goals: information should be available to those authorized to use it, but some types of information should not be circulated freely. For computer systems, however, data access and manipulation involve programs, operating systems, operating personnel, and interconnected hardware components. Each computer may store a vast amount of information, and these data may be shared by all machines within a network. The range of security issues, therefore, must extend to each of these areas as well as to the data themselves.

A review of these issues naturally begins with security matters within a single machine. The problems are generally similar to those in earlier times, although the nature of electronic media adds subtleties and sophistication. New difficulties arise, however, when the discussion turns to interconnected networks of computers. Many old problems still arise, but opportunities for security violations are much harder to control. Ultimately, security in any age depends upon the actions of people and how they handle the responsibilities and trust they are given.

═══ INTRAMACHINE ISSUES ═══

The simplest computer environment for handling computer security involves a single-user machine with no internal, long-term storage, e.g., a personal computer with no hard disk drive. Here, each user must bring his or her own programs and data to the machine, and nothing is stored within the machine when it is turned off between users. Each person takes responsibility for his or her material, and personal diskettes either accompany the individual or may be locked in a drawer or cabinet.

With such a simple system, many security issues parallel earlier times. Insiders may carry data or programs with them as they move from place to place; outsiders may attempt to break into buildings, vaults, and cabinets; diskettes may be left unattended in places where others may take or copy them.

Beyond these traditional problems, physical threats to computers extend well beyond fire and water. Disk drives may break; diskettes may become damaged; magnetic or electronic fields may destroy data or programs; power surges may damage hardware; programs or systems may malfunction, erasing or destroying data. Such possibilities for harm, of course, rarely affect information in paper form, and special precautions and procedures are needed for safeguarding information within computers. For example, backup copies of data and programs are routinely made, so information can be retrieved from a backup copy even if a diskette becomes damaged or if a system malfunctions. When diskettes or other storage devices may contain the equivalent of hundreds or thousands of pages of material, such backup of information is particularly important. Multiple copies of data reduce the chances that a simple malfunction will result in the loss of data, but clearly multiple copies of a data set compound the traditional difficulty of controlling access to data.

═══ MULTI-USER MACHINES ═══

Whenever several people may use the same machine at the same time or whenever data or programs from several users are stored on the same machine, authorized use become much more complex. Ideally, one might hope that user programs and the computer's operating system would limit access to restricted data, but in practice there are many ways unauthorized users might obtain information.

A particularly simple way to transmit data from one person to another uses files. One user may create a data file with sensitive data, this file may be placed in long-term storage (e.g., on a hard disk), and another user then may read or work with the file. Such a scenario is not unlike the more traditional practice of letting another person borrow a file folder. Unlike past times, however, one cannot always look at a computer to see duplicated files – a careful search of files throughout a computer may be required. Solutions to this potential for sharing files typically follow one of two basic approaches.

1. Files may be identified as belonging to individual users or groups of users. Access to information then depends upon a listing of who may access what.

2. Information within files may be encoded, so that only authorized individuals will be able to understand what is stored. Anyone may read a file, but the data will appear as a muddled mess to those without the capability to decode the information.

Passwords. Limiting access to data requires that a computer distinguish one person from another. For example, each user may be given a separate computer account and password. The system then operates under the assumption that each individual knows his or her password, but others do not. Data are then restricted when a potential intruder cannot supply the required access code.

Unfortunately, password systems often work better in theory than in practice for several reasons.

- Since users do not want to forget their own passwords, they often choose codes which are easily guessed. Common favorites include their own names or nicknames (sometimes repeated twice), names of relatives or friends, well known dates (e.g., birthdays, anniversaries), and popular words or phrases. For example, some studies have found that as many as 40% or 50% of the passwords on a system may be guessed following a few very simple rules and guidelines.

- Users may tell their friends about passwords, so a friend may use a particular program or data set.

- Even if non-mnemonic names are chosen, users may post passwords next to their workstations, so they won't forget what to type. Of course, others will find this posted information equally helpful.

- Passwords may be sufficiently short that they may be determined by simple trial-and-error. (Until recently, for example, one business used a system where passwords for all users consisted of exactly two capital letters.)

- Since a computer must store password information somewhere, system flaws, operator errors, or procedural mistakes may allow current users access to this file. Numerous stories tell of lists of current passwords appearing on terminals or printers, for example.

- Most computers allow system managers special privileges, so the machines may be run smoothly and so updates and operations may be performed effectively. In such situations, managers normally have the power to peruse all files on a system, regardless of password protections that might inhibit other users.

- If outsiders or regular users are able to break into a manager's account, then these people too can examine and modify all files. (In one system known to this author, an administrator was worried about forgetting the manager's password, so left it blank. Individual accounts were well protected, but anyone who merely tried to log in as manager had no trouble whatsoever obtaining special powers with a privileged status.)

Overall, then, passwords have the potential to limit access to information, but any such system must be used carefully, following well-established protections and procedures. Carelessness may open such systems to a wide range of abuses.

Data Encoding. A second way to protect data is to encode them, so only authorized can make any sense of the information present. With the processing power of modern machines, programs sometimes encode data automatically before every store operation and decode all information before it is displayed to an authorized user.

With encoding and decoding, of course, the level of security depends upon the ciphering system actually used. During the times of the Gallic Wars, Julius Caesar encoded messages to his troops by replacing each letter by the third letter after it in the alphabet. Applying this idea to the modern English alphabet, 'a' would be encoded as 'd', 'b' as 'e', and so forth. At the end of the alphabet, 'w' would be coded as 'z', 'x' as 'a', 'y' as 'b', and 'z' as 'c'. While this system, now called a *Caesar Cipher*, seems very simple, the code was never broken by Caesar's enemies, and it served as a secure form of communication.

Today, the art and science of cryptanalysis has become very sophisticated, and simple codes such as a Caesar Cipher can be broken very quickly and easily.[1] Secure codes must be much more sophisticated.

The Caesar Cipher, for example, has at least two major weaknesses. First, since every letter is coded by the third (or fourth or nth) letter after it, once the code for one letter is determined, the codes for every other letter also are known. To illustrate, consider the coded message

```
Igkygx iovnkxy gxk kgye zu ixgiq
```

and suppose you know (or guess) that this has been sent using a type of Caesar cipher, but you do not know if the shift is one letter or two letters or three or more.

To decipher the message, you could simply try each of the 26 possible shifts of the alphabet and see which line makes sense. In the case of the message above, the choices are shown below:

Shift by	Alphabet Coded By	Possible Decoding of Message
0	ABCDEFGHIJKLMNOPQRSTUVWXYZ	Igkygx iovnkxy gxk kgye zu ixgiq
1	BCDEFGHIJKLMNOPQRSTUVWXYZA	Hfjxfw hnvmjwx fwi jfxd yt hwfhp
2	CDEFGHIJKLMNOPQRSTUVWXYZAB	Geiwev gmtlivw evj iewc xs gvego
3	DEFGHIJKLMNOPQRSTUVWXYZABC	Fdhvdu flskhuv duh hdvb wr fudfn
4	EFGHIJKLMNOPQRSTUVWXYZABCD	Ecguct ekrjgtu ctg gcua vq etcem
5	FGHIJKLMNOPQRSTUVWXYZABCDE	Dbftbs djqifst bsf fbtz up dsbdl
6	GHIJKLMNOPQRSTUVWXYZABCDEF	Caesar Ciphers are easy to crack
7	HIJKLMNOPQRSTUVWXYZABCDEFG	Bzdrzq bhogdqr zqd dzrx sn bqzbj
8	IJKLMNOPQRSTUVWXYZABCDEFGH	Aycqyp agnfcpq ypc cyqw rm apyai
9	JKLMNOPQRSTUVWXYZABCDEFGHI	Zxbpxo zfmebop xob bxpv ql zoxzh
10	KLMNOPQRSTUVWXYZABCDEFGHIJ	Ywaown yeldano wna awou pk ynwyg
11	LMNOPQRSTUVWXYZABCDEFGHIJK	Xvznvm xdkczmn nmz zvnt oj xmvxf
12	MNOPQRSTUVWXYZABCDEFGHIJKL	Wuymul wcjbylm uly yums ni wluwe
13	NOPQRSTUVWXYZABCDEFGHIJKLM	Vtxltk dbiaxkl tkx xtlr mh vktvd
14	OPQRSTUVWXYZABCDEFGHIJKLMN	Uswksj uahzwjk sjw wskq lg ujsuc
15	PQRSTUVWXYZABCDEFGHIJKLMNO	Trvjri tzgyvij riv vrjp kf tirtb
16	QRSTUVWXYZABCDEFGHIJKLMNOP	Squigh syfxuhi qhu uqio je shqsa
17	RSTUVWXYZABCDEFGHIJKLMNOPQ	Rpthpg rxewtgh pgt tphn hd rgprz
18	STUVWXYZABCDEFGHIJKLMNOPQR	Qosgof qwdvsfg ofs sogm ic qfoqy
19	TUVWXYZABCDEFGHIJKLMNOPQRS	Pnrfne pvcuref ner rnfl gb penpx
20	UVWXYZABCDEFGHIJKLMNOPQRST	Omqemd oubtqde mdq qmek fa odmow
21	VWXYZABCDEFGHIJKLMNOPQRSTU	Nlpdlc ntaspcd lcp pldj ez nclnv
22	WXYZABCDEFGHIJKLMNOPQRSTUV	Mkockb mszrobc kbo okci dy mbkmu
23	XYZABCDEFGHIJKLMNOPQRSTUVW	Ljnbja lryqnab jan njbh cx lajlt
24	YZABCDEFGHIJKLMNOPQRSTUVWX	Kimaiz kqxpmza izm miag bw kziks
25	ZABCDEFGHIJKLMNOPQRSTUVWXY	Jhlzhy jpwolyz hyl lhzf av jyhjr

With this approach, a simple trial-and-error process produces the actual message with little difficulty. (In this case, 'A' was coded 'G'.)

Second, using a Caesar Cipher, every letter in the actual message is encoded by the same letter in the cipher alphabet. This allows people trying to break a code to take advantage of statistical properties of English. While there can be variations among different texts, 'E' is usually the most frequently used letter, with 'T' second, and so forth.[2] Thus, another approach to breaking a code (given enough text to study) is to count the number of times each coded letter occurs. The chances are quite good that the letter appearing most frequently will be a 'E' or 'T', for example.

Approaches to Improve the Caesar Cipher. With these basic weaknesses in the Caesar Cipher, improvements may be made in several basic ways. First, instead of simply replacing a letter by the third (or nth) letter after it in encoding, the letters of the code might be scrambled, as in the following example:

Plain Alphabet: A B C D E F G H I J K L M N O P Q R S T U V W X Y Z
Cipher Alphabet: R V I N T O Q F Z P A X H B K D C J W U M E Y G L S

Here, each letter in an actual message can be replaced by the corresponding letter in the cipher alphabet, so that 'FUN' is encoded by 'OMB'. This approach resolves the first major deficiency in the Caesar Cipher, since a knowledge of part of the code ('O' stands for 'F') does not appreciably help decipher other parts of the code.

The second deficiency is often addressed by following one of two approaches. In the first approach, a different code may be used for each subsequent letter in the message. Thus, to encipher 'FUN', the letter 'F' may be enciphered using one cipher alphabet, 'U' using a second, and 'N' using a third. Certainly, if this approach is used, with a different coding scheme for each letter and if the pattern of coding schemes is changed for each message, then the messages may be unbreakable. However, as a practical matter, such an approach is unwieldly. Both the sender and the receiver must agree on the sequence of codes to be used, and management of many different codes can be difficult.

Thus, in practice, it is not uncommon to use one basic cipher alphabet, but then to use different shifts for subsequent letters. For example, one might agree that the first letter would be coded by the cipher alphabet, shifted by 3 letters (as in the original Caesar Cipher), the next letter shifted by 1 letter, the next by 4, then by 1, 5, 9, 2, 6, 5, 3, 5, etc. (where this sequence of shifts may be remembered as the digits of the mathematical number π.)

To simplify the logistics further, the pattern of shifts might be repeated after a certain number of letters. For example, once the first eight letters are coded by shifts of 3, 1, 4, 1, 5, 9, 2, 6, then the next eight letters also might be coded by the same pattern of shifts.

Codes produced in these ways are much better than the simple Caesar Ciphers. The simplifications needed to manage the logistics of such approaches, however, also can open potential weaknesses that may be exploited by cryptanalysts (those trying to break the code to obtain the underlying data). Statistical methods used for single alphabet codes often may be extended to these multiple cipher approaches, at least when patterns repeat or when they can be predicted.

Another major approach for resolving problems of statistical analysis of letters involves coding several letters at once, rather than coding letter-by-letter. For example, a code could be constructed, so that pair of letters were coded. (Perhaps 'ED' would be coded by 'RM'.) With this approach, counts of individual letters would not give much information to potential cryptanalysts, since the code was not based on such individual letters.

Even here, however, when reasonably large amounts of text can be collected, patterns may be observed and statistical analysis of groups of letters may provide insights. Coding pairs of letters may create some difficulties for cryptanalysts, but these are rarely insurmountable.

Increasing the size of the groups, however, can greatly complicate the work required to break a code. When 50 or 100 letters are encoded as a group, for example, the task of cryptanalysis may be sufficiently time-consuming that codes can be cracked only after many years (at which time, the data may no longer be sensitive or even relevant).

This approach of encoding reasonably large groups of letters is the basis for one of the most popular of today's encryption schemes, called **public key systems**, which are often used with modern computer systems. Such systems typically involve three main elements.[3]

First, each group of letters is interpreted as a number n. (If a group had only one letter, we might consider 'A' as 1, 'B' as 2, 'C' as 3, etc.)

Second, the number n is put into an arithmetic formula to get a coded form. For example, the formula might specify numbers e and m, so that the coded number c is $c = n^e \bmod m$. That is, the word's number n is raised to the power e, and the remainder is computed after dividing by m. With this approach, c is easily computed.

Third, when e and m have been chosen carefully, it turns out that a similar formula may be used to decipher the message. In particular, there may be a number d where $n = c^d \bmod m$. The security of the code then depends upon the difficulty of computing d (and m). For a public key system, a person wishing to receive coded messages will publish m and e, so anyone can send him or her information. The coding scheme is straightforward, fast (at least when machines do the computation), and public. On the other hand, under certain circumstances, the computation of d may be expected to require so much time that data will remain secure for a long time.[4]

With such systems, there is always the possibility that a new discovery or insight will suddenly allow d to be computed easily and quickly from m and e, but this is beyond the capabilities of current knowledge. Thus, this approach currently is viewed as reasonably secure, at least if m and e are chosen carefully.

Communication between Accounts. Unfortunately, even limiting access to accounts and files does not guarantee that data on multi-user machines will be safe. At least three other types of risks may be considered:

- Programs accessing data may make additional copies of the material. A particularly surreptitious program, for example, could copy data to another user's account as it was doing its work for an authorized user. An intruder then could obtain information by just waiting for an authorized user to access it.

- After files are edited or copied, old versions may remain. To be complete, erasing should involve two steps: First, disk or file space should be overwritten, so no sensitive data remain. Second, the space previously occupied by the data may be deallocated, so it may be used again. (Translating these steps to paper files, paper should be shredded before it is recycled.)

  Unfortunately, on many systems, only the second step is performed. Overwriting disk files is time consuming, and this step may be omitted. In such cases, information can be obtained by looking through space recently deallocated. (Again, in a paper world, this is not unlike looking for information by searching through someone's trash barrels.)

- Two programs running on the same processor may communicate, either directly or indirectly. For example, a process using sensitive data might send messages to another person's program running at the same time. Alternately, when messages are not sent directly, processes may take advantage of the scheduling of work by the operating system within a computer to transmit data.

While this communication between accounts or programs may be reasonably complex and certainly requires some collusion, such possibilities may arise whenever users share a single machine. Overall then there are many ways that unauthorized may obtain sensitive data through clandestine or defective software as well as by sloppy file handling. Multi-user machines, therefore, have considerable potential for allowing the unauthorized distribution of data and programs.

═══ INTER-MACHINE ISSUES ═══

When individual processors or computers are linked to a network, the potential for security leaks expands significantly. The problems already identified for single processors remain, but small difficulties on a single processor may be used as wedges to open wider leaks in a distributed system. In addition, some new types of problems may arise.

Wire-tapping. At a physical level, any network of machines must use some medium to transmit data from one place to another. When all electrical components are physically close to each other, such communication may be monitored carefully by security personnel to prevent unauthorized individuals from connecting to the transmission medium and copying information as it is sent. As distances become longer, however, such physical observation becomes much more difficult. For example, exposed wires and junction boxes may be tapped, radio waves may be intercepted, and electromagnetic fields from electrical cables may be monitored. In the latter two cases, data may be captured without any physical connection to a wire. With such opportunities for eavesdropping and wire tapping, data can no longer be considered safe simply by locking them in a vault. Outsiders may have an opportunity to receive data as they move from one place to another in a network.

Coordinating Processor Security Levels. Even when physical channels are secure, interprocessor security is complicated since different people normally have different capabilities and requirements on different machines. As a simple example, someone with a personal computer at his or her home or office may have complete freedom to access and modify anything on that system. The owner may work with all data and programs at will, with virtually no constraints. When that machine is connected to a network (perhaps so the homeowner may work with material needed at the office), then the office machine may limit the information available through the personal computer.

As the needs of users expand through a network, each machine must monitor who is allowed to access what data, and different levels of users may enjoy different privileges. In many cases, at the deepest level, each machine may have to trust what it is told by others in the network. For example, a request for data may include the identity of the user, and a machine receiving the message may need to assume the user's identity is correct.

Frequently, on large systems on national networks, a person with special system privileges on one machine may be given expanded privileges on another connecting machine. If the person is responsible enough for one system, the assumption may be made that he or she will be equally trustworthy on the next system. Such an assumption may be shaky, but to limit such privileges too much could greatly restrict the usefulness of the network and the ability of responsible workers to do their work. On the other hand, granting such privileges also aides an intruder on one system in gaining access to other systems in a network. If a person breaks into one machine (perhaps by guessing a password), that person may be able to then try to break accounts on connecting machines.

In a related problem, the possibilities for guessing passwords may be enhanced on distributed systems. As a simple illustration, if one machine can interact with a second, then the first simply might try to log into an account on the second by trial-and-error. If an account name is known, for example, the first machine could simply try all possible passwords, one after another. Such a brute force approach could take a very long time if an account's password was a random collection of characters, but the process might go quickly if a user had chosen a simple word or name. (To reduce such possibilities, many systems will stop accepting attempts to log in if passwords are consistently wrong, or alarms may be triggered to warn of attempted break ins.)

On other systems, such as the widely used UNIX[5] operating system, user account names are stored in public files with encoded passwords. While deciphering passwords may not be feasible, users on a system can use the system to encipher words. In such a setting, common words can be enciphered and then checked against all passwords in actual use. Whenever a code matches, one knows the password on the given account. Thus, anyone with access to an account may be able to search through passwords to gain access to some other accounts as well.

In general, gaining access to one machine or to an account in one machine often opens up many ways to break into other accounts.

Trojan Horses. Another approach that often expands a person's capabilities involves the exploitation of generally accessible file areas. For example, commonly used programs may be grouped together in a directory that many people can access. Similarly, routine administrative tasks may be done automatically by running programs stored in special locations.

If security measures within a system are somewhat lax, however, a clever user might be able to introduce a new program into such a system area, and this program then may be run automatically as part of administration or accidentally by another user. If such a program were to copy sensitive data or grant special privileges, then the original user might gain access to restricted information. Such programs are called **trojan horses**, and unfortunately stories of security violations due to such trojan horses are quite common.

Viruses and Worms. Two other types of subversive programs that can undermine system security and reliability are viruses and worms. The mechanics of these programs differ in their operation and in the ways they spread through a system, but the ideas in each case are reasonably similar. Each case affects the functioning of an operating system by entering a machine from a source that is trusted to be secure. Once within the machine, the program is run and it affects the further operations of the machine. Sometimes the effects may be harmless, but in other cases data may be lost or modified, or a system may be unable to continue functioning. In each case, system security has been breached, and system users may no longer know what operations and data are reliable. (A few years ago, one major company shut down its computer operations on a Friday the 13th due to rumors of difficulties that might occur when that date was reached.)

Viruses – typically are transmitted on diskettes that are used on one machine and then another. When any diskette is inserted into a machine, some initial data are read to tell the computer about the type of material present. If this initial information is altered in certain circumstances, the computer may be instructed to change its programs, data, or mode of operations. Details depend greatly upon the particular machine involved and so are omitted from this discussion.

Worms – typically enter machines over network communication channels that are considered reliable. A worm takes advantage of weaknesses in one system to transmit itself to other machines, where the program may be duplicated and retransmitted. Again details depend upon particular networks and machines.

In many cases, both worms and viruses are designed to perform some unusual or clandestine operation, and such activity may include telling the computer to make additional copies of themselves. These additional copies may then be run to cause further deterioration of a system or network. Sometimes this duplication process has the potential to destroy a great deal of data or to bring normal operations to a halt. As in medicine, a single virus program (or cell) may be relatively harmless by itself, but as it reproduces to produce more copies of itself, the result can overwhelm the health of a system.

Example: Stalking the Wily Hacker. Some possibilities for several types of security leaks are demonstrated particularly well in a celebrated case described by Clifford Stoll.[6]

In his commentary, Stoll reports that an intruder gained access to the Livermore Berkeley Laboratory (LBL) computers in August 1986. While trying to track down the identify of this person over the following ten months, Stoll (with the support of LBL and the help of personnel at other sites) followed this individual's attempts to break into about 450 other computers. More than 30 of these attempts were successful. More specifically, Stoll reported that half of the 450 attempts were unsuccessful because the computers were unavailable. Of the remaining 220 attempted log ins,

- 5 percent were refused by a distant computer (set to reject LBL connects [no one at LBL was allowed access to these machines]),

- 82 percent failed on incorrect user name/passwords,

- 8 percent gave information about the system status (who, systat, etc.),

- 1 percent achieved limited access to databases or electronic-mail shells,

- 2 percent yielded normal user privileges and a programming environment, and

- 2 percent reached system-manager privileges.[7]

Thus, about 5 percent of the attacks against Internet computers were reasonably successful. In this case, the intruder was particularly interested in military or classified information, and one might expect computers involved in such applications to be more secure than machines used for general computing. It is not unreasonable to expect that the percentage might be higher for machines with more general uses. In the same article, Stoll compares his results with other, independent studies of attempted break-ins to systems and concludes, "break-in rates of 3–20 percent may be expected in typical network environments."[8]

Such rates suggest that while many computers may be somewhat resistant to intruders, persistence can pay off. Different attacks on the same machine, trying different user names and accounts or taking advantage of different characteristics of a system can allow an outsider to find holes and to take advantage of potential weaknesses. For example, in reviewing this work of the intruder, Stoll writes

> The intruder conjured up no new methods for breaking operating systems: rather he repeatedly applied techniques documented elsewhere. Whenever possible, he used known security holes and subtle bugs in different operating systems, including UNIX®, VMS®, VM-TSO®, EMBOS®, and SAIL-WAITS. Yet it is a mistake to assume that one operating system is more secure than another: Most of these break-ins were possible because the intruder exploited common blunders by vendors, users, and system managers.[9]

The intruder also guessed account names and passwords to gain access to other accounts and machines. Overall then, the intruder gained access to a wide range of computers around the world by taking advantage of many of the potential security problems mentioned in this chapter, including software errors, easily guessed passwords, and procedural errors. Throughout this work, potential weaknesses were present in each system, and the person methodically took advantage of these circumstances. As Stoll reports,

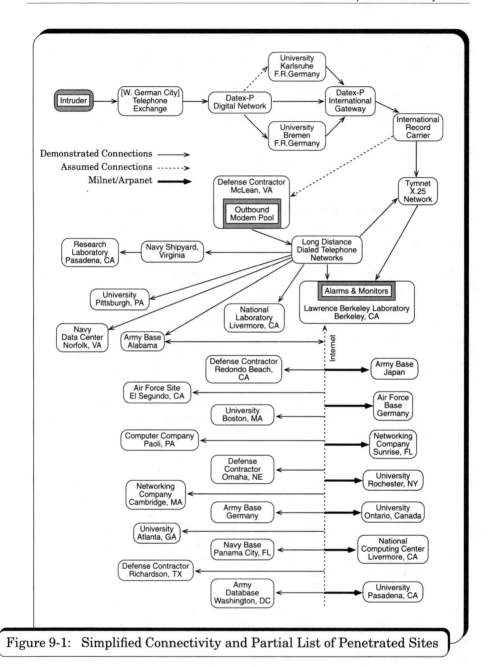

Figure 9-1:   Simplified Connectivity and Partial List of Penetrated Sites

"the person we followed was patient and plodding, but hardly showed creative brilliance in discovering new security flaws."[10]

With these relatively well-known techniques, the scope of the intruder's activity is impressive. As shown in Figure 9-1, the intruder lived in Germany and used the local telephone exchange to obtain access to a nearby machine. This computer then allowed this individual to enter various national and world-wide networks. (Long distance charges were borne by some of the installations under attack.) After several stages, the intruder was able to connect to the LBL computers (where monitoring of his activities started), and this gave the intruder access to the Internet for access to many machines and networks throughout this country. Figure 9-1 also shows clearly the diversity of machines and the range of locations that may be involved with interconnected networks.

As a postscript to this story, it is worthwhile to note that the identity of this intruder finally was determined only through a long-term, concentrated effort by Clifford Stoll and others. Various monitoring and tracing capabilities could be utilized in the work, but tracking the individual took great effort and resourcefulness. The presence of an intruder was first determined in investigating an accounting error, for the intruder had created a new account with no corresponding billing number. Access to this accounting information was obtained when the intruder took advantage of a subtle error in a standard text editor and was then able to gain system manager privileges. In tracing the results, printers were attached to users' lines to read everything the intruder typed, activities were constantly monitored, and telephone calls were traced. While further details are beyond the scope of this book, the interested reader is encouraged to read the full account in one of the sources listed in the notes. The complete story of the monitoring and eventual identification of the intruder makes fascinating reading.

═══ TRUST: A CATCH-22 OF COMPUTING ═══

While there are many ways that unauthorized people may attempt to gain access to sensitive data, each potential security leak often can be closed once it is identified, and the regular monitoring of systems can usually keep possible leaks closed.

For example, attempts to wiretap or otherwise physically break into a system can be controlled by regular searching and monitoring of cables leading between machine components. Coaxial cables can shield data transmission lines, so electrical fields cannot be detected. Boxes containing wire connections can be locked and monitored.

On the other hand, while such measures are possible, some can be quite expensive. For example, for a large distributed network with workstations scattered over a wide area, the costs to assure such physical security may be prohibitively high. In practice, therefore, perfect physical security may be unrealistic; costs may be unacceptably high for the potential benefits, and some risk may seem appropriate. (In cases where radio transmission is used for data communication, such physical security may be completely impossible.)

Similarly, on a small scale, every diskette on a personal computer could be reviewed and tested each time it was inserted into a drive to scan for viruses. On the other hand, a user may find that such constant testing is a considerable nuisance, and such testing may be limited or omitted in practice.

These examples illustrate the basic problem that security safeguards often can be effective only when potential hazards are identified and systems monitored. Wire junction boxes may be secured, but constant monitoring may be needed to guarantee that new attempts at wiretapping will be thwarted. Programs can test diskettes for the presence of known viruses, but they may not be very helpful against newly created ones.

Historically, leaks normally are plugged only after successful break-ins have been identified and safeguarded. Security measures often respond to new, innovative ways to obtain unauthorized information, and complete security can be quite elusive.

Enforcing Security. Effective security of programs and data relies on a wide range of techniques. While many opportunities are available for breaking into files and obtaining unauthorized data, many can be thwarted by appropriate procedures, programs, tests, monitors, and patrols. Even with these measures, however, security depends upon how carefully and reliably the measures are implemented and how carefully security issues are reviewed. Ultimately, some collection of people, hardware, and software must be trusted.

To move this general issue of trust to a more concrete level, consider the following questions, which may also give some indication of the magnitude of the related issues of trust and security.

• When you use a word processing package, how do you know that the program is not making another copy of what you type, so that copy could be accessed by someone else? (Any program you run will have access to your files, of course, since you are the one running it, and you certainly can access your own files.)

• In a related matter for a program with several users and printers, when you ask the machine to print some information, how do you know that the operating system or the print procedure does not make a copy at the same time, perhaps printing the copy on another printer?

• If you buy new software for your personal computer (perhaps you purchased a new word processor, spreadsheet, or video game), how do you know that the diskette containing the software does not contain a virus? (Some commercially available packages have been contaminated in the past.)

- If you use a virus checker on your own personal computer, how do you know that it works as claimed? More generally, how do you know any software package does what it claims? How can you be sure that something odd will not happen when the package is run a certain number of times?

- When you log on to a large computer system, how do you know that the operating system is not displaying your password to someone else? How do you even know that the log-in process is genuine, i.e., not being simulated by some other program that is designed to capture your password or to copy your files?

- When you call a service or repair company, how do you know that the person who comes to your business has not attached a wiretap to your data communication lines?

- In a bank environment, how would you detect if a programmer in the computing department had added a piece of code that would allow his or her account to be overdrawn? Similarly, in computing interest to the nearest cent, how would you know that any extra fractions of a cent were not credited to the programmer's account? (This latter event has happened, where the total amount of interest accumulated checked out correctly, but the programmer became rich by getting thousands of fractions of a cent daily whenever interest for any account was computed.)

- If your computer has a modem that can connect it to telephone lines, how do you know that some piece of software does not automatically call a toll-free number (or a local number) periodically when no other processing is occurring to transmit updates on data files?

While some readers may be able to give specific answers to some of these questions, it is humanly impossible for anyone to check personally all of the software that is used on any computer system of any size. Even a relatively well established software package might contain some security problem that has not been publicized or perhaps even identified. And yet, programs with thousands of lines of code cannot possibly be reviewed by every user or even by every system manager. The scope and complexity of computing systems, therefore, requires that users trust someone (e.g., managers, software and hardware vendors, maintenance personnel, operators) to monitor processing and to anticipate, detect, and eliminate security problems.

Unfortunately, whenever one relies on trust at some level, there is always the possibility for unscrupulous individuals or groups to take advantage of the circumstances. As a result, it is virtually impossible to ever be completely sure that any computing system of any size is completely secure.

═══ SUMMARY ═══

The Internet is a national computer network,[11] designed to aid the distribution of materials, and as with any network, the Internet depends upon some level of security to ensure that it will work smoothly. Each facility connected to the Internet expresses a level of faith in the system.

Since the Internet involves many machines (roughly 60,000 in the Fall of 1988), it was particularly newsworthy when, between November 2 and November 4, 1988, the Internet was the target of a worm[12], which spread rapidly through the network and infected a large number of machines nation-wide. While this worm did not contain any code that intentionally destroyed or altered data or programs, it did disrupt operations on many machines in computer centers around the country. While the ramifications of this worm are still being discussed, this worm provides a particularly good example of many of the issues of computer security that have been discussed in this chapter.

- Once it became established on one computer, the worm tried to spread to other machines in several ways.

- The worm identified machines connected to the current one by looking at various lists of network interfaces and computers.[13] Such lists are publicly available to facilitate the exchange of information.

- The worm tried to run itself directly on such nearby machines, hoping that the current machine had permission to work directly with others.

- Computers on the Internet often contain a mechanism to determine the names of their valid accounts. This greatly simplifies the sharing of information between users, since one person can look up the account name of others before sending materials to that account. On the particular systems under consideration, a flaw in the look-up mechanism (called *fingerd*) allowed the worm to plant a program on the new computer that resulted in the worm being copied to the new machine.

- In sending messages between machines, it is often convenient for system managers to be able to verify mail is arriving at its destination correctly without their having to log on to the new system. Thus, the *sendmail* facility for sending messages has a *debug* mode that gives people on other machines some special capabilities. While this presents some security risk, the *debug* mode is often left on for convenience at many installations. When on, however, the worm could use this mechanism to start itself up on new machines.

- While general users or managers could not move freely from one machine to another, there was always the possibility that an individual might have accounts on several machines. In such cases, often the individual would use the same password on each machine. Alternatively, one account might be set up so that once the user was on one machine, he or she could log directly onto another without having to give his or her password again.

- The systems in question stored passwords in encrypted form, so no one could determine passwords directly, and there was no reasonable way to decipher these passwords. On the other hand, the worm was set up to take advantage of human nature in several ways:

  1. The worm tried some obvious choices of passwords (e.g., the null password and names made out of the account name).

  2. Based upon some experimental results, the worm tried a list of 432 words that computer users choose frequently.

  3. The worm used the English dictionary available on each system for checking spelling. For each word in the dictionary, the worm enciphered it following the encryption system used for passwords and checked the result against all encrypted passwords.

Whenever the worm could break into an account by any of these methods, the worm then tried to use this user's capabilities to log onto any related accounts on other machines. If any of these attempts were successful, the worm could then copy itself to the new machines and start the process again.

Overall, the worm targeted specific computing systems by taking advantage of both weaknesses of human nature (in selecting guessable passwords) and specific flaws in commonly used computing environments.

═══ CONCLUSIONS AND IMPLICATIONS ═══

Computer security involves granting authorized personnel access to confidential or sensitive data, while preventing others from using this same information. For some simple, isolated computer systems, this problem often may be solved reasonably well, for the machine can be placed behind locked or guarded doors, where only appropriate people may get near it. Once several users have access to a machine, however, problems multiply. For example, terminals and wire connections may be tapped, passwords may be circumvented, errors in software may be exploited, and procedures may be ignored. When several machines are interconnected on a network, such problems are only compounded further.

Certainly, the examples and references cited in this chapter suggest that no computer should be considered completely safe and secure. One study indicated, for example, that break-ins might be successful between 3 and 20 percent of the time on typical network machines. While such rates might discourage the casual or informal observer, there is every reason to believe that determination and persistence will pay off. Security procedures, hardware, and software may slow an intruder down, but such prevention measures should be expected only to delay break-ins, not eliminate them.

Computer systems simply are too complex for one person or even one group of people to be able to control and monitor all aspects of the system, and some potential leaks will be present. Given time, persistent or clever outsiders will be able to gain access to data in any networked system without authorization; any assumption to the contrary is almost certain to be incorrect.

══ DISCUSSION QUESTIONS ══

9.1 Discuss whether or not it is ethical for a student or employee to write a password-guessing program?

    a. How would you respond to the argument that a password-cracking program provides an intellectual challenge?

    b. If a student is successful in learning the password of another student or an instructor, should the student be punished for reporting to the other student or instructor that his or her password is not secure?

9.2 On many machines connected to national networks, "guest" or "anonymous" accounts are established to allow people from around the country to log on to the machines. With such accounts, anyone can log on to a machine without having to know a password. Typically, the capabilities available from such accounts are somewhat restricted, but they do allow interested users to locate, copy, and edit publicly available data and to run programs. Such sharing of data can support a wide range of research and development efforts, and much educational software and materials are exchanged at low cost through such opportunities.

While "anonymous" accounts can aid legitimate access to publicly accessible data, they also can provide a convenient starting place for people wishing to obtain sensitive data. Review various ways of obtaining unauthorized access to data on distributed networks, and describe at least two major ways that such "anonymous" accounts could be used in breaking into restricted data or accounts.

9.3 One way the problem of trust is complicated for computers is that a very large number of people may have a legitimate responsibility for part of a system. Determine what capabilities each of the following people should be given in order to do their jobs, and consider how each of them might use those powers to obtain or transmit unauthorized information if they wished.

- Computer Operators

- Software Developers

- System Managers

- Repair/Maintenance Personnel

- Users on a Multi-User Computer

9.4 Suppose a programmer teamed up with a member of a testing or system administration group. Describe a few ways (at least two) where the two could work in collusion to obtain sensitive data in a way that would be difficult to detect. For example, how could one person cover for the other?

9.5 This chapter ends with the sentence, "it is virtually impossible to ever be completely sure that any computing system of any size is completely secure." In view of the possibilities for unauthorized access to data described in this chapter, evaluate whether you think this sentence is overly guarded, overly pessimistic, or about right. For example, consider the following questions:

- Is the statement overly guarded; could the word "virtually" be omitted? In other words, can you describe any reasonably-sized computing system that could be guaranteed to be secure? How would you know it did not have security leaks?

- Is the statement overly pessimistic or alarmist; would it be more accurate to state, "While it may be somewhat difficult, it is quite feasible to create and operate a secure computing system."

Justify your answer.

9.6 The March 20, 1989 issue of *Time* magazine (pp. 25–26) discusses the potential for security violations within networks of computers within the military. For example, *Time* reported that "the U. S. arrested and expelled a military attaché for allegedly trying to steal details of computer-security programs." The article then considers the following hypothetical scenario.

> • An enemy agent in the Pentagon sends a computer virus through the World-Wide Military Command and Control System, which the U. S. commanders would rely on in wartime for information and coordination. The virus sits undetected. When hostilities begin, the agent sends a message that triggers the virus, erasing everything in the system.

> • A different virus is introduced into NATO's logistics computers. Triggered just as the Soviet army marches into West Germany, the virus alters messages so that all allied supplies are sent to the wrong places. By the time the mistake is corrected a day or two later, key parts of NATO's defense line have collapsed.

a. Discuss some ways that such a virus might be injected into such a computer network. Who might be able to plant the virus? How?

b. How could the possibilities for this type of threat be reduced or prevented?

c. *Time*'s article states that "officials differ about the likelihood that such sabotage could be carried off." What do you think? Justify your answer.

9.7 A manager of a computer system may need to restrict the privacy of users in order to preserve system security, which in turn is required to guarantee all users' privacy.

a. Give some examples to illustrate the potential conflicts that can arise when restricting privacy in order to guarantee security.

b. How might the need to maintain computer system security conflict with constitutionally guaranteed rights and freedoms?

c. Develop some guidelines that may help resolve this conflict.

NOTES

1   For an interesting account of a variety of simple techniques for breaking codes, see Abraham Sinkov, *Elementary Cryptanalysis, A Mathematical Approach*, The New Mathematical Library, Random House, New York, and the L. W. Singer Company, 1968.

2   Sinkov, *op. cit.* presents more frequency count information on p. 16.

3   For more information, see Donald W. Davies, *Tutorial: The Security of Data in Networks*, IEEE Computer Society, Los Angeles, California, 1981. The discussion here follows the general treatment given in Part II of Davies' tutorial, pp. 115–134.

4   In one popular version of a public key system, developed by Rivest, Shamir, and Adleman, m, e, and d are obtained as follows: One starts with two large prime numbers, p and q. Then let $m = pq$ and let $L = lcm(p-1, q-1)$, the least common multiple of $p - 1$ and $q - 1$. Then d and e may be computed by taking any solutions to the equation $de = 1 \bmod L$. While such computations are easy once p and q are known, the discovery of p and q is difficult given only n, since the factoring of very large integers can require a large amount of time and energy. While further motivation for such work and the reasons this works are beyond the scope of this book, details may be found in Davies' *Tutorial*, already cited, or in the original paper, R. L. Rivest, A. Shamir, and L. Adleman, "A Method for Obtaining Digital Signatures and Public-Key Cryptosystems," *Communications of the ACM*, Volume 21, Number 2, February 1978, pp. 120–126.

5   UNIX is a registered trademark of AT&T UNIX System Laboratories.

6   Stoll writes a fascinating account of his efforts to track down an intruder to the Livermore Berkeley Laboratory computers in his article "Stalking the Wily Hacker," *Communications of the ACM*, Volume 31, Number 5, May 1988, pp. 484–497. His story has also been described in a program produced for Public Television. Various other accounts of this material have also appeared in several publications.

7   *ibid*, p. 494.

8   *ibid*.

9   *ibid*, p. 484.
UNIX is a registered trademark of AT&T Bell Laboratories.
VMS is a registered trademark of Digital Equipment Corporation.
VM-TSO is a registered trademark of International Business Machines Corporation.
EMBOS is a registered trademark of ELXSI.

10   *ibid*, p. 485.

11   The Internet links thousands of machines located in academic, business, and government facilities around the country. For example, the vast majority of all colleges and universities in the United States have machines that can access

this network, either directly or indirectly, for the use of faculty, students, and administrators. Over the years, this network has been particularly helpful to researchers and developers collaborating on projects and sharing results. Drafts of research papers are circulated for review and comment; new versions of software packages are distributed; ideas for classroom lectures, laboratories, and presentations presentations are communicated; queries may be broadcast concerning experiences or understandings that others may have had for particular situations; and a wide variety of educational materials are available to all interested parties. Such a network represents many of the best qualities of a network, and a tremendous amount of worthwhile work has come about because of opportunities for communication on the Internet.

12   In January 1990, a jury found Robert Morris, Jr., guilty of introducing this worm, and on May 4, 1990, Federal District Judge Howard Munson fined Morris $10,000, required that he engage in 400 hours or community service, placed him on three years probation, and required that he pay some additional administrative expenses. (It is reported that his legal costs were much higher than the fine itself.) At the time of this incident, Morris was a graduate student at Cornell University.

13   Since the worm needed to take advantage of specific weaknesses in specific machines, it targeted a commonly used operating environment, specifically variants of the UNIX operating system that ran on either VAX computers (manufactured by Digital Equipment Corporation) or Sun 3 systems (manufactured by Sun Microsystems). The details that follow, therefore, are specific to that environment. However, similar weaknesses may be anticipated on virtually any machine, and the lessons apply generally to any network.

PART V
Conclusions

If architects built buildings the way programmers build programs, then the first woodpecker to appear would destroy civilization.

—From Anonymous ATM graffiti.
Quoted by Bryan Kocher, *Communications of the ACM,*
Volume 32, Number 6 (June 1989) p. 660

"We make no warranty or representation, either express or implied, with respect to the software described in this manual, its quality, performance, merchantability, or fitness for any particular purpose. As a result, the software is sold 'as is,' and you the purchaser are assuming the entire risk as to its quality and performance. In no event will we be liable for direct, indirect, special, incidental, or consequential damages resulting from any defect in the software or manual, even if we have been advised of the possibility of such damages."

—From standard disclaimer of a major software vendor,
reported by the *Computer Professionals for Social Responsibility*

People display a remarkable tolerance for computer systems. Imagine a car manufacturer that used this guarantee for its automobiles. In effect, it says, "We don't stand behind our cars, but you are welcome to risk riding in it." This seems to be a classic case of the traditional view *caveat emptor*, "let the buyer beware." In today's world, such a business could hardly expect to continue in operation for any length of time. Buyers expect a reasonable level of quality from builders of appliances, drug manufacturers, and food producers. Laws protect consumers from snake oil remedies and various false or exaggerated claims.

And yet, vendors of computer systems are not held to the same standards. Consumers or users often expect computers to malfunction. In many contexts, "the computer made a mistake" is an acceptable excuse. Of course, some systems work extraordinarily well, and there are spectacular successes in computing applications. Unfortunately, failures sometimes are equally spectacular, and computers take the brunt of many jokes and accusations.

While such accusations and claims sometimes may be false or exaggerated, this book has identified a wide range of limitations and constraints. Chapter 10 reviews this evidence and reaches some important conclusions.

CHAPTER 10

A Dead Fish

Fred Finn Mazanek, a one-year-old guppy, died recently, leaving an estate of $5000.

A student at the University of Arizona received one of the computer-mailed "occupant" life insurance offers. The student diligently filled out the insurance form for this fish, listing the fish's age as six months, his weight as thirty centigrams, and his height as three centimeters. Another computer (or maybe the same computer who mailed the original offer) duly issued Policy No. 3261057 in Fred Finn's name from the Globe Life and Accident Insurance Company and began billing and collecting premiums.

A few months later, the fish died, and the owner filed a claim. Although the insurance company was quite upset, they found it best to settle out of court for $650.

—From Dennie and Cynthia L. Van Tassel, *The Compleat Computer, Second Edition*, Science Research Associates, Inc., 1983, p. 22.

Piano Sale

The Allen Piano and Organ Company of Phoenix advertised by radio that its computer had made a mistake in ordering inventory; the company was overstocked and was therefore holding a sale. A member of the Association for Computing Machinery called the company and offered to fix the faulty program free. He found out that the Allen Piano and Organ Company did not have a computer and had not been using any computer facilities. The "computer error" was just a sales trick.

—From Dennie and Cynthia L. Van Tassel, *The Compleat Computer, Second Edition*, Science Research Associates, Inc., 1983, p. 233.

The Role of Computers

Although difficulties and limitations may be inherent in computing, the recent history of computers indicates, of course, that computers can help solve a very wide range of problems. This record of success indicates that some obstacles of computing do not always occur, while others may be overcome adequately in certain circumstances. On the other hand, this book suggests that it may not be possible to resolve all difficulties related to specific computing applications; some obstacles are fundamental.

Many successes of computers share some common qualities, and a review of these provides a broad context for considering computing limitations. A balanced perspective on the use of computers acknowledges both the potential for computers to help solve problems and the practical and theoretical limitations inherent in working with these machines.

═══ WHAT COMPUTERS ARE GOOD AT ═══

At a very basic hardware level, computers perform three primary types of operations on data: the storage and retrieval of data, the comparison of different data items, and the arithmetic or logical manipulation of data. All of this work is done following specified instructions. Computers can be particularly effective when applications require a significant use of one or more of these operations.

Example: Word Processing. Word processing and desktop publishing provide a good illustration of how the capabilities required in an application mesh nicely with the characteristics available in computers. Word processing largely involves at least two types of work. First, any manuscript involves text – the words (and possibly the diagrams or pictures) that form the raw data for the composition. This text must be stored and retrieved, and much of the value of using a computer for word processing arises from this data storage. When drafts of a manuscript are stored, editing can take advantage of information already present; only modifications must be noted, and much of the composition can remain without changes. Without the computer's ability to store and retrieve data, computers would be of little value in word processing applications.

Second, word processors provide capabilities to format text, including such possibilities as changing margins, justifying lines, changing fonts, and aligning equations. Each of these tasks involves the logical manipulation of data. (When spelling checkers are used as well, heavy use also is made of a computer's ability to compare words with dictionary entries.)

Beyond these basic data operations, word processing has the important characteristic that each word processing task can be described carefully, completely, and precisely in logical terms. For example, justifying a line involves adding spaces between words to make both the left and right margins align properly. To perform this task, a computer can determine both how much space to add and between which words the extra spaces may be inserted. While this process requires some sophistication and subtlely to ensure that every page will look balanced and attractive, such details can all be reduced to a basic list of rules.

This ability to identify the rules needed for formatting text illustrates two, more general characteristics for the successful development of computer applications. First, the task of word processing can be described fully; complete, unambiguous specifications can be written for the application. Second, given the specifications, detailed algorithms are available to perform the desired tasks efficiently. There is little question about what to do or how to do it. Since the task of publishing has been performed for centuries, people have considerable expertise in solving the wide variety of problems that can arise in typesetting and composing a manuscript. The primary advantage of using a computer is that machinery can perform these long, tedious, repetitive tasks quickly and accurately.

In light of the discussions earlier in this book, word processing also has some additional properties that can contribute to it being a successful computer application.

• Word processing relies heavily upon relatively few capabilities that are used very frequently. This constant use of the same features exercises specific parts of a word processing program, so normal use provides an excellent testing environment. A typical typing session will involve the same editing and formatting sequences over and over again, and any programming errors therefore are likely to be found reasonably quickly.

• While users might like word processing (including formatting and printing) to be done efficiently, this processing is not usually done under severe time constraints. For example, adding a few minutes to the printing of a document is unlikely to be a critical factor in the value of a word processor. (There may be constraints on how fast a user may enter text into the processor, but details of type fonts and printing may be less severe.)

• In many word processing applications (other than in the creation of form letters), users normally proofread their work and make corrections. This provides a natural, built-in monitoring process that can help identify situations when a word processor malfunctions. Further, with frequent use, typists or editors may learn ways to get around or resolve known errors or peculiarities in a word processing package. Users learn to live with processing difficulties, and special problems are naturally identified as part of the proofreading process.

To summarize, the following properties combine to make word processing a particularly good application of computing:

- The application has well defined, precise specifications.
- Word processingdraws upon strengths of computers, namely
    the storage and retrieval of data and
    the manipulation of data.
- The work environment provides an excellent opportunity for extended testing.
- The interaction between machine and users allows constant monitoring of results; users can correct errors naturally, as part of their work.
- This application does not have severe time constraints; constant review and revision of results is practical.

Example: Weather Forecasting. Weather forecasting illustrates a second area that makes particularly good use of computers. Initially, weather forecasting involves monitoring instruments that record current conditions, determining such factors as temperature, wind speed and direction, visibility, and precipitation. Such readings are taken at many observation sites, both on land and in the air (through the use aircraft, balloons, satellites, etc.), and such information currently gives a good description of weather. Since this phase of work requires the accumulation and storage of massive amounts of data, computers are very well suited for this data acquisition phase of meteorology. Computers can continually monitor sensors and store readings. Further, data can be scanned for reasonableness and consistency with nearby readings, and this can help identify malfunctioning hardware.

As a next step, well understood principles of physics (e.g., fluid dynamics) can be applied to project where various weather systems will move and how those systems will affect future weather conditions. While the details require a deep understanding of a range of scientific specialities, the relevant points for this discussion are:

1. Forecasting depends heavily upon applying detailed mathematical formulae to massive amounts of data; and

2. The accuracy of the forecasts generally is increased as the number of observation sites increases.

This second phase of forecasting also meshes nicely with the capabilities of computers to perform computations efficiently and in a timely manner.

Computers are effective at number crunching, and forecasting is worthwhile only if the millions of computations can be performed quickly.

To be somewhat more precise, forecasting normally proceeds by dividing a geographical region into relatively small blocks in a three-dimensional grid, and data are collected for at least one point in each block. As an analogy, one might think of a house as being divided into rooms, and one might record the temperature and humidity in each room to get a general picture of the comfort level of each location in the house. A more precise picture might include variations of temperature within a room. However, one might divide the room logically into four or more section and take readings in each area. These additional readings, for example, might show the locations of drafts of cold or hot air.

To determine weather patterns, computations are made for each block (or room or section of a room) following well-known formulae. General trends can be established when these formulae are applied repeatedly to determine changes every six hours or every day. More accurate and detailed computations can be made if changes are noted every hour or every fraction of an hour. Throughout the work, the same formulae are used, but accuracy depends upon dividing the area in question into reasonably small graphical regions and computing projected weather conditions at each piece at frequent intervals (every hour or less).

In comparing this computer application to word processing, both share some common properties, although forecasting makes significantly more use of the computer's computational capabilities. To summarize, the following properties combine to make weather forecasting a particularly good application of computing.

- The application has well defined, precise specifications.
- Algorithms (formulae) are well established from physics.
- The processing required meshes nicely with the strengths of computers, namely the storage and retrieval of data and the heavy use of arithmetic.
- Accurate forecasts require massive computations, which cannot be completed by hand in a timely manner.
- There is considerable opportunity for the extended testing of programs and data. Input data can be monitored for problems with sensors. Output data can be compared with known models. Predictions can be compared with the actual conditions that occur later.
- Constant review and revision of results is practical.
- People can review predictions before warnings are issued.

Many of these characteristics apply to a broad range of successful computer applications.

═══ **LIMITATIONS** ═══

While computers have capabilities that can be very helpful in solving problems, this book has emphasized that computers also have limitations. Some constraints are practical; ways may be found to resolve some or all of them. On the other hand, some limitations are more fundamental; one can prove that these difficulties cannot be overcome. The following list highlights some of the main issues identified in earlier chapters.

- *Specifications:* One cannot know if the specifications for a problem are complete and consistent. In tackling complex problems, therefore, one cannot be sure one is considering the right problem.

- *Problem Solving:* Even when a problem is stated, one cannot always be sure the problem has a solution.

   Unsolvability: Some problems have no solutions; they are unsolvable.

   Nonfeasibility: Some problems have no feasible solutions; solutions may exist, but they cannot be completed in a reasonable amount of time, due to computational consequences of the combinatorial explosion.

- *Hardware:*

   Reliability: While hardware tends to be more reliable than software, unanticipated hardware malfunctions can occur, with possibly serious consequences.

   Speed: While continued improvements and refinements in hardware speed are possible, past advances in computer speeds cannot continue at the same rate, due to limitations in the speed of light.

- *Software:* Error-free software is not achievable for complex systems.

   Development: Every stage of the software development process, including determination of specifications, algorithm design, coding, and testing, provides many opportunities for mistakes, oversights, and errors.

   Reliability: Every large-scale software package has errors. Some may be known, but one should expect to find new errors, even in programs that have undergone extensive testing.

Maintenance: Maintenance of existing software has a reasonable likelihood of introducing new errors, even if its purpose is to correct known errors. Not all errors, therefore, should be corrected.

- *Simulations:* All simulations are based upon models, and such models in turn depend upon assumptions (either stated or unstated). Results of simulations, therefore, can only be as good or valid as the assumptions that underlie them.

- *Human Error:* Human error can be expected in the entry of data and in the operation of computer systems. This introduces mistakes even when portions of a system normally run properly.

- *Security:* While computer security can involve both physical and electronic measures (e.g., both hardware and software), such measures are only as good as the people who develop and monitor them. Security requires putting one's trust in developers, maintainers, and managers.

Overall, these issues can generally be classified into two types of problems: theoretical and practical. Theoretical problems are fundamental. Logical arguments show that certain problems are unsolvable and that others have no feasible solutions; speeds cannot exceed that of light. Unfortunately, no amount of work or effort can resolve these obstacles to developing computer systems.

Practical problems are more difficult to categorize. Some practical problems, such as determining whether specifications are complete and consistent, may be unsolvable. Other practical problems may be solved or their effects reduced. For example, some difficulties of writing specifications, developing algorithms, and producing computer programs can be eased through computer-assisted design (CAD) and other technical tools. Such techniques cannot be expected to solve all such problems, but the use of modern tools may help reduce the number of such difficulties.

The effective planning and developing of computer systems requires a consideration of both types of limitations. When practical problems are encountered, ways must be found to compensate for the difficulties. Procedures and capabilities must be available to handle errors made by hardware and software, when they arise. When theoretical problems arise, however, no amount of work can solve the problem posed, and alternatives must be found. For example, if one could show that no technical solution is available for defending against a nuclear attack, then one alternative might be to find a political way to eliminate nuclear weapons. When technical solutions are unavailable, one must avoid the problem.

==== SUMMARY ====

1. Computers can perform three types of data operations effectively: the storage and retrieval of data, the comparison of different data items, and the manipulation of data.

2. Computers may excel in applications that take advantage of these operations.

3. Other characteristics, such as the opportunity to monitor output and results, also may be helpful in assuring the success of an application.

4. Computers also have a variety of limitations. Some constraints are based on theoretical or logical arguments, while others arise from practical considerations.

5. The range of limitations and constraints is very broad, involving such areas as specifications, problem-solving (with both unsolvability and nonfeasibility limitations), hardware (with both reliability and speed constraints), software (development, reliability, and maintenance), simulations, human error, and security.

6. These factors combine to yield the conclusion that for any complex system, one must assume that:

   - the specifications that form the basis for the system are flawed,

   - the hardware and/or software contains errors,

   - software errors will be compounded by human error in data entry and system operation, and

   - the system will be vulnerable to breaches in security.

==== CONCLUSIONS AND IMPLICATIONS ====

In reviewing these issues, several conclusions seem appropriate. First, there is no reason to assume that one can find appropriate, feasible solutions to difficult problems. Some problems can be proven to have no solutions; some are known to have only nonfeasible solutions. Such possibilities should be considered whenever the development of new systems is contemplated. When a problem, such as the Halting Problem, has no solution, no amount of funding and effort will produce a satisfactory resolution to that problem. Feasibility studies must allow for such possibilities.

Second, much of the work in developing and verifying computer systems depends upon the writing of specifications. Reviews of code, the development of tests, and the formal verification of code using mathematical proofs all depend upon specifications, but one can never be certain that a list of specifications is complete and consistent. Various automated tools can help find omissions and inconsistencies in stated specifications, but the absence of known errors does not imply that no such mistakes actually exist. Further, even if specifications could be shown to be free from such problems, questions arise as to whether systems following the specifications will actually resolve the desired problems. Unfortunately, specifications depend upon individuals' perceptions of a problem, but there is no effective way to know if those perceptions are accurate. Overall, while the writing of specifications forms the basis for the work of developing systems, this foundation can be quite weak. Further, if subsequent work or experience finds significant errors within the specifications, the entire structure of the system can crumble and fall apart.

Third, any system must maintain a balance between work that is done automatically and work that is monitored by people. Complex computer systems always have errors: their specifications may be incomplete or incorrect, their algorithms may be wrong, the software itself may contain mistakes, or the hardware may malfunction. To resolve such problems, people must have the capability to make corrections; people must be able to work with the system at all levels to fix mistakes. On the other hand, people also can make mistakes when working with machines: data can be mistyped, and people may operate equipment improperly in a variety of imaginative ways. Computer systems may anticipate some types of these problems, and checks may be included to help prevent some such difficulties. Overall, these difficulties lead to a constant tension for designers. The possibility of computer error suggests that people be given considerable responsibility and control in running a system, but the possibility of human error suggests that people be constrained in what they are allowed to do.

Fourth, computer system security depends upon the proper working of both hardware and software and upon the constant use and monitoring of security mechanisms. People must take advantage of protections built into systems, those mechanisms must function properly, and action must be taken when alarms or other reporting devices indicate possible security breaches. Unfortunately, difficulties can be anticipated with each of these areas. There is a long history of computer users and administrators circumventing security measures, since such measures may require special operations or activities for users. Security mechanisms themselves rely upon the proper functioning of hardware and software, and this book has described numerous problems that commonly arise with each of these areas. Monitoring takes time and effort, which naturally can interfere with other concerns and interests that people have. While any one of these factors can produce gaps in security, all of these difficulties combine to support the conclusion that no computer system should ever be considered to be completely secure; security can never be assumed to be complete. Further, the larger the system and the more legitimate access there is to that system through a variety of workstations and computers, the more opportunities there are for difficulties with security and the less confidence one should have about security. On large distributed systems, containing many computers and workstations, a combination of factors make it likely that unauthorized users will be able to access either software (programs) or data or both.

These limitations and constraints suggest that provision must always be made for systems to go wrong. Errors should be expected in hardware, software, data, and operations. Breaches of security are always possible. Thus, the planning for the design and use of any system must include both an analysis of the risks of such problems and a series of plans and procedures to follow when these difficulties arise. Both theoretical and practical considerations lead to the conclusion that malfunctions, either intentional or inadvertent, will occur in complex systems. The issue in using computer systems, therefore, is how to respond to such problems.

═══ DISCUSSION QUESTIONS ═══

10.1 Classify each of the limitations reviewed in this chapter as to whether it is primarily a practical problem or whether the difficulty is more fundamental (there is no way to remove the obstacle).

10.2 The first anecdote at the beginning of this chapter describes two common computer applications: computer-generated mail and automated processing of mail orders. The second anecdote mentions a sales pitch commonly heard on radio and television. Do these stories have any broader implications? What do these stories suggest concerning the role of computers? Explain your answer.

10.3 Each of the following paragraphs describes a computer application. In each case, determine some characteristics of this computer application, and compare these properties with the list of things computers can do well. Then, review this application in the light of the limitations of computing outlined in this book. What are the risks inherent in using computers in this context? Are there steps that can be taken to minimize those risks?

a. A fighter aircraft may fly at speeds that are so fast that people cannot respond in time to avoid or correct various conditions. (By the time a pilot decides to turn to avoid another aircraft or a missile, for example, a collision may already have occurred.) Thus, much of the control of such an airplane is often turned over to a computer, where the response times can be quicker.

b. In a hospital, sensors attached to a computer may be used to monitor patients in a critical care ward. This allows constant review of a patient's vital signs, and it provides a mechanism to alert medical personnel if a patient's condition changes abruptly.

c. Extending the application in (b), the computer may be attached to devices that can administer drugs and that can take other preventive or corrective measures. For example, a drop in a patient's blood pressure might signal the need to administer a drug intravenously.

10.4   Since each of the applications in question 10.3 involves hardware and software built by humans, each has the possibility of the computer system malfunctioning. In each case, describe what might go wrong. Then consider who might be responsible for the problem? (For example, who might be legally or morally liable?)

10.5   One policy that has been discussed for defending the United States against a surprise attack involves the concept of *launch-on-warning*. Under this policy, sensors (radar, satellites, reconnaissance planes, etc.) constantly monitor the skies for evidence of an enemy attack (presumably using missiles and/or aircraft). When sensors determine that such an attack has started, planes and missiles are launched immediately to retaliate.

Proponents of a launch-on-warning policy point out that missiles can travel across the world in a very few minutes (perhaps 15 or 20 minutes). Thus, the United States has only a short time to retaliate before an enemy attack could eliminate much of the capability of the United States to respond. Thus, effective retaliation may be possible only if the response begins before the enemy missiles and/or planes reach their targets. Times simply are too short to allow a lengthy review of possible attack data, and the consequences of an attack may be too devastating to ensure a reasonable response after the attack is completed.

Opponents of a launch-on-warning policy point to the potential for error in a response and the consequences of responding incorrectly.

a. Review this launch-on-warning approach in the light of known capabilities and limitations of computer systems.

b. Take a stand on this policy, either for or against, and write a strong argument supporting your conclusion.

10.6 If you were offered the ultimate managerial responsibility for SDI (the star wars defense system), would you take it in light of the limitations and potentials for computing outlined in this text? Assume that the financial rewards would be great. What would influence your decision?

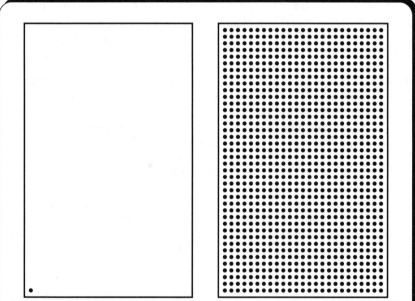

The single dot on the left represents the amount of code in the Unix™ operating system (approximately 10,000 lines). This code is operational, although not completely bug-free. The dots on the right represent the amount of code projected for the Strategic Defense Initiative or "Star Wars" (approximately 10,000,000 lines). It will have to work flawlessly the first time.

Computer Professionals for Social Responsibility
P.O. Box 717, Palo Alto, CA 94301

Figure 10-1:   Projected Code for the Strategic Defense Initiative

10.7 The organization, Computer Professionals for Social Responsibility, or CPSR, takes stands on a variety of social, ethical, and technical issues related to computing. Figure 10-1 shows a poster prepared by CPSR to oppose the Strategic Defense Initiative or SDI.

    a. Using the library or other resources, determine some of the goals of SDI, and review these goals in view of the capabilities and limitations of computer systems.

    b. On the basis of this review, discuss whether you believe the CPSR poster in Figure 10-1 is fair. Does the poster make a relevant point or does it distort the issues? Justify your answer.

    c. Suppose that you headed a software development firm, and suppose that you were offered the contract to be the primary contractor for SDI software. The contract presumably would employ a great many people, you could expect to earn a very high salary as head of the project, work on the contract would allow your firm to tackle many interesting technical questions, and successful completion of the project might contribute to national security. On the other hand, technical questions might or might not be solvable, possible solutions might not be feasible, and errors in any stage of the software development process could have dramatic consequences. Would you accept the contract? Explain your decision, using in part your answer to part (a).

A Short, Annotated Bibliography

David Bellin and Gary Chapman, *Computers in Battle – Will They Work?*
Harcourt Brace Javanovich, 1987.
An investigation of various roles that computers play in the military, together with an assessment of their quality and reliability. As noted on the book's jacket, this book "presents the scientific and technological facts as well as expert analysis of this controversial subject in a readable, non-technical style." The presentation touches on many issues identified as limits to computing, including problems in writing specifications, design and coding algorithms, testing, maintenance, reliability, redundancy, security, and human factors.

Nathaniel S. Borenstein, *Programming As If People Mattered: Friendly Programs, Software Engineering, and Other Noble Delusions,* Princeton University Press, 1991.
A reasonably light, easy-to-read introduction to issues concerning the interface between the computers and users. Since users interact with computer systems directly through such interfaces, this subject can be central in determining how effectively a system can be used, how likely users are to make errors, and how easy such errors are to correct. The book offers many insights on the development of good user interfaces, including both good experiences and unfortunate systems. For example, the book examines some of the tensions between managers and developers, and illustrates how compromises may arise in the development of software.

Frederick P. Brooks, Jr., *the mythical man-month*, Addison-Wesley, 1975.
A classical text on issues in software engineering, which is most readable and entertaining. (Some people have described it as pleasant bedtime reading.) The author served as the project manager for the IBM System/360 and OS/360 project, and thus has gained many insights both on how to organize and construct large software systems and on what can go wrong. This book provides valuable insights about practical considerations that should be part of any software development project.

Peter J. Denning, editor, *Computers Under Attack: Intruders, Worms, and Viruses*, ACM Press and Addison-Wesley, 1990.

An anthology of articles describing a variety of threats to computer security, with examples and case studies. The book examines a wide range technological, socio-political, ethical, and legal issues.

David Gries, *The Science of Programming*, Springer-Verlag, 1981.

The classical textbook on formal program verification. This book contains considerable depth in the subject and requires some mathematical sophistication. The first chapters develop the rigorous, logical machinery required to prove that programs are correct. These tools are then used in conjunction with programming to write code that works correctly the first time. The reader needs to work at least through chapter 16 to see many of the benefits of this approach.

Peter G. Neumann, editor, "Risks to the Public in Computer Systems," a consistent section in *Software Engineering Notes, An informal Newsletter of SIGSOFT, the Special Interest Group on Software Engineering*, published bimonthly by ACM, the Association for Computing Machinery.

Reports many accidents and incidents related to the malfunctioning or misuse of technology and is a wonderful source of examples. Comments and notes often tie specific occurances with more general principles.

Abraham Sinkov, *Elementary Cryptanalysis, A Mathematical Approach*, The New Mathematical Library, Random House and the L. W. Singer Company, 1968.

A widely-distributed presentation of many simple techniques for breaking codes using elementary probability and statistics. This book provides considerable insight into what makes some encoding schemes secure, while other approaches may be rather easy to break. For national security reasons, few advanced texts are available to the general public.

ACM Journal of SIGCHI, the Special Interest Group on Computer / Human Interfaces

An excellent resource for exploration of the topic of Graphical User Interfaces (GUI's).

Henry M. Walker, *Computer Science 2: Principles of Software Engineering, Data Types, and Algorithms*, Scott, Foresman and Company, 1989.

A presentation of several topics related to the *Limits of Computing*, at a medium level of technical detail. The text is designed for the second semester of an introductory computer science course sequence and thus assumes some familiarity with Pascal programming. Chapters 1 and 3 expand themes involving software engineering, Chapter 12 considers program correctness and accuracy, Chapter 13 discusses complexity theory and NP-Completeness, Chapter 14 introduces elements of hardware and operating systems, and Appendix B describes some common ways data are represented within computers.

Index